Mr C Wood
The Manor House
1 Owthorpe Road
Cotgrave
NOTTINGHAM
Nottinghamshire
NG12 3JE

DONINGTON OAK

POEMS

GILLIES SHIELDS

Published in Great Britian
by
WILTON 65
Flat Top House, Bishop Wilton, York. YO42 1RY
2000

Paperback ISBN 0947828850
Caseback ISBN 094782880X

This book is dedicated

'to my wife Ann'

PREFACE

Gillies Shields and his family are well known in Leicestershire. Born in Breedon Hall at Breedon-on-the-Hill in North West Leicestershire in 1919. Apart from 14 years abroad while in the Army and in East Africa, he has played a leading role in country life in Breedon and neighbouring Castle Donington, inheriting historic Donington Hall and Estate in 1943 while serving in Abyssinia. The Army had occupied the Hall and Estate in 1939 and did not release it until 1956, when he returned from East Africa and began a 10 year restoration plan of the Hall, Estate and Farms. Great improvements were made but, unfortunately, death duties and lack of capital prevented fulfilment of his aims. The Hall was lent rent and rate free to refugees from Hungary, the Baltic States and Displaced Persons Camps which he had seen in Germany, and he helped organise and run the place for a decade. During this time he was an active farmer, Chairman of the Parish and R.D.C., a J.P., church warden, President of Local Agriculture Society and British Legion and Rutland Polo Club and on many Boards and Committees.

A passionate defender and advocate of all aspects of country life and sport and a local historian, he has been able to express his local knowledge and beliefs in imaginative prose. His poems about Breedon-on-the Hill and Donington Park show his love for the area; and his epic *Donington Oak* reflectsthe changes through the years as seen by one of the ancient oak trees standing in the Park. A Celtic Idyll harks back to the days when the Coritani Celts made their home there. His sense of romance led to his love poems, some with a hint of despair. He writes about his Beliefs in serious mood, but then follows these with some lighthearted and nonsense verses.

As with most people caught up in its horrors, the War years left a deep impression on Gillies Shields. When he was commissioned, it was said that as a 17 year old, he was the youngest officer in the British and Empire Forces since the First World War. He has been able to record some of his experiences after six years of service with his county regiment, seldom out of action. His heroic Norway Saga was appreciated by the King of Norway, and is said to have been accepted by the Norwegian military academy.

Some of Gillies poems, as well as various other articles, have appeared previously in journals and magazines, such as *The Leicester Graphic*, *Derbyshire Countryside*, *The Rose Annual*, and *Country Life*. He is also the author of *Old Tom of Tooley, Father of the Quorn* published in 1998 to celebrate the 300 years of the Quorn Hunt founded by Thomas Boothby in 1698. The first two editions were sold out within six months and a third edition is being contemplated.

Acknowledgement:

'to Frank and Christine Agar for their willing and unpaid work on a word processor.'

Donington Oak Poems
Gillies Shields

Poems about Breedon-on-the-Hill, Leicestershire

Poems about Donington Park, Leicestershire

Love Poems

Epics

Miscellaneous

Tonight - Song

Gail - Written at Donington Park Farm overlooking
Breedon-on-the-Hill with its ancient Church on top.

Tonight I stand in sullen pride
And watch the Wilson vale,
And wish that I could gently glide.
Above the fields so pale
And down to Staunton Harold slide
Or top of Breedon sail,
And lie there on the cradle tower
And dream of dark-eyed Gail.
Tonight the moon's magnetic power
Has caught the Nightingale
Whose songs unveil each lover's bower,
And haunt each whispering dale;
As she regales the world asleep
All beauteous things can't fail
To wake and wonder why I weep
With longing for my Gail.
Tonight the wind begins to sweep
The branches with its flail
And soon the boughs will bend and break.
And bow down to the gale
The farmhouse hums and rafters quake
And wires begin to wail,
Yet none of this keeps me awake
But only thoughts of Gail.

1960

THE GRAVEYARD

At Breedon-on-the-Hill

The words engraved upon the stones
In deathbeds old as sin
Are breathing tales of buried bones
Bereft of blood and skin.
These cocoons of the Christian soul
Are hollow to our eyes;
But that which went before is whole;
The spirit seldom dies.
And round us as we weekly walk
To keep our faith alive
We pass these silent tombs that talk
On both sides of the drive.
Like office registers, these scrolls
On graves record the stay
Of guests in life's hotel. And holes
Below are bins of clay
In which their dusty scraps are laid.
Do passing traveller's die
When Ink upon the bill marked "paid"
Is dry? They cry "goodbye"
And hail the cab of change. So these
Are granite leaves in God's
Accounting Book. And with the breeze
That fans the greeny sods,
Transcendent souls swim round the waves
Of singing bells and heed
The organ's thrill They see their graves
As but the husk of seed,
Or like the milk teeth of the young
Discarded in the pain

Of growth; for man has many a rung
To climb to Heaven's plane.
They watch us in our passing breath
And speak with soundless signs
To cells within ourselves. For death
Unlocks the door to shrines
Of Eden's peace where man is born
Again without the birth
In pain, or tears, or night, or morn,
Or any of the storms on earth.

1960

SUNSET

*On ** Breedon-on-the-Hill*

The sun is settling down for bed
And shedding off her rays;
She blushes coyly crimson red,
Undressing to our gaze;
And softly, now, her drowsy head
On cloudy down she lays,
And overall is slowly spread
The shawl of night. She stays
Awake awhile to watch stars shed
Their sheltering light and pays
Her homage to the moon whose thread
Of beams, like arms ablaze,
About her bed keeps guard. Now dead
Asleep she lies and day's
Delight dies with her dreams. Instead,
The moon now rules the maze
Of cosmic eyes, till dawn, when lead
Becomes light foil and greys
And silvers, gold. The moon has sped
With cloak unfurled; the haze
Unfolds, the sun shakes off the dread
Of the night to rise with sprays
Of song from skies. For night has fled
And birds awake with praise.

1938

*** The author was born at Breedon Hall*

4

THE RIVER TRENT AT KINGS MILLS

"I never feel a bliss so pure and still,
So heavenly calm as when a stream or hill,
Or veteran oak, like those remembered well.
Or breeze or echo of some wild flower's smell
(For who can say what small and fairy ties
The memory flings o'er pleasure, as it flies!)
Reminds my heart of many a sylvan dream
I once indulged by Trent's inspiring stream:
Of all my sunny morns and moonlight nights
On Donington's green lawns and breezy heights"

Thomas Moore

At Swarkestone Bridge the water wends so silently and slow
As though afraid to waken sleeping swans, or rouse the cows
From dreamy browse; and bends between the fields of green to flow
Towards the Wiggs where herons perch and preen on poplar boughs:
Below them lie the deep lagoons where lurk the perch and pike
And cunning carp, and tench, and roach and where the barbel, bream
And dace abound. The Wiggs, that once were drained for sport, with dyke
And flight and punt-gun ponds and sluice and shaven rides, now seem
A wilderness, gone wild when man was forced to fight in wars.
Unruly nature has run riot and ruined the ordered scene
And left a land bereft of form; but full of burrs and briars
And bulrush blades and reeds and marsh; a mangrove swamp of green
And yellow catkin tails, of hazel wands and willow palms
Among the roots of fallen trees. The creatures of the ground
And air proclaim their bounds with Courtship songs; the dusk alarms
As pheasant cocks alight to roost, the drumming snipe, the sound
Of sneezing grunts the roding woodcock makes, the curlew's cry,
The call of cootes, of greylag geese, the moorhen and mallard drake,

5

The shoveler, teal, and tutted duck, the whistling golden eye,
The doves and pigeons plaintive cooes, and nestling herons crake.
The river runs now very wide as past the park she glides
And creatures that have slept by day awake to hunt by night.
The tawny and the long eared owls fly out their oak tree hides
To float and skim the countryside with eyes that see in light
Or dark, the moves of mice; their hoots and woos and 'ki-wik' cries
Conjoin with mews of little owls that flit and dip from tree
To tree, to scoop up shrews and slugs and beetles, bugs, and flies
And tiny birds. And, like a ghostly kite that's broken free,
The barn owl, white in face and breast, patrols the moonlit dales
And shoots with eerie shrieks on rodent prey. The sparrow hawk
And kestrel, too, are seen and heard around the woods and vales
Of Donington, as Trent, beneath the shade of boathouse walk,
Her mazy current pours. The dog fox snaps his warning bark
As after rats he stalks the park and takes to cubs in different dens,
Dispersed for safety's sake, their food. He sprays his scent to mark
His own domain on stumps and posts and nettle clumps. No pens
A keeper makes are safe, no farmers' hens or ducks will sleep
If left unlocked at night, and wise men watch their sheep by day
When ewes are due to lamb. And from their setts the badgers creep
And bring out bedding, soiled below, to spread some yards away.
With grunts they root around for grub, and young cubs play tag-tail
And catch-me-if-you-can. Sometimes the air is rent with fear
As when a keening vixen screams, a piercing, strident wail
Of woe that tells of tortured souls in hell. And one can hear
The fallow deer in season fight and antlers clash as foes
Dispute a rutting stand with belching groans and troats from deep
 within their throats. The prickets play around as docile does
Contently feed and pay no heed to fighting bucks and keep
Away until the victor calls. The red stags are engaged
Also in desperate duels and horns are locked as placid hinds
Ignore the jousts. The river is arrested now, encaged
Into channeled flow where man with might have changed its course

To work his water mills. But now the will of man has waned
And wheels can work no more. The water flees with freedom's force
Escaping down the broken weirs leaving the mill-race drained
And dry. The Melbourne castle stairs of stone can only weep
As down the breach the waters plunge. The ancient paddle wheels
Now paralysed of power will sleep till rust. The famous salmon leap
Is but a memory of less polluted times. The trap for eels
No longer yields its weekly wagon load for London town.
The foaming Trent rejoins the prehistoric way it went
Before the weirs were built, and leaves the mills to settle down
In beauty's lap to rest at peace, content.

Notes

1   The poet Thomas Moore visited Donington Park and Kings Mills
many times between 1799 and 1827 to see his Patron, Lord Moira,
later 1st Marquis Hastings, or to use the library at the Hall. He wrote
several poems about the Park and the Trent.

2   The weirs at Kings Mills were repaired by the Earl of Huntingdon
from the stones of Melbourne Castle, thus fulfilling a prophecy that
one day the Waters of the Trent would overflow the towers of
Melbourne Castle.

THE PARVENU

The ivy crawls up crumbled walls
That mark the entrance to the Park.
The stumps of Ash and Oak recalls
A canopy of leaves as dark
As dusk and trunks as tall
As giant's stilts when, as a lad,
I stood within the wood to call
The pheasants for their food. I'm sad
To see just stumps there now and weep
To be where once the ornate lodge
Had been, that keeper's wife would keep
So clean and neat. Now rabbits dodge
Between the nettle-beds and docks,
A wilderness of green and piles
Of bricks. And badgers dig up blocks
Of carved sandstone and coloured tiles
And crockery and Swithland slates
That once adorned the lodge that graced
The gravelled drive. The massive gates
Of wrought iron lace have been replaced
By cattle-grids. The stump lined drive
Is concrete now; the avenue
Of ancient limes did not survive
The chainsaw gang the Parvenu
Employed to rationalize his grand
Estate. The park seems naked, shorn
Of all its trees and deer; the land
A prairie now of rape and corn.
The Hall is shamefully exposed,
Undressed for all to see. With scorn
She sees a swimming pool imposed

Upon her lawn; her insides torn
And twisted round and turned to small
Apartment blocks. The Squire is dead;
So tread with care, for when Squires fall
Sometimes the trees fall too. Shed
A tear, for when Squires die the Hall
Can die of grief if strangers show
No sympathy for beauty, age
And family. When Squires go
So goes a rural heritage.

THE BARN

At Park Farm, Donington Park

It makes me sad to see the way
We let our ancient barn decay.
The garnered grain no longer lies
Inside the granary but dries
In grim silos of tin. The loft
Where lay the meadow hay, so soft
And sweet, is strewn with cans of spray
And fertiliser bags. The straw and hay
Is wrapped in plastic rolls and piled
Outside. The fragile roof, pan-tiled
And warped, is still rain-proof and keeps
The rafters dry. The barn owl sleeps
In cavities beneath the eaves,
and acts the farmer's friend and leaves
At eventide to glide for rats
And mice. And from the beams the bats
Still hang and flitter down at night
To catch nocturnal moths in flight.
The medieval mellow brick
Has weathered well; the walls are thick
And bulging at the waist like man
In middle age. Unlike the van
That rots nearby, the barn is just
As natural as the Oak and must
Be spared the blade. It blends as though
It grew as slow as acorns grow.
For here were held the great wassails,
The ox roastings with warm spiced ales,
And harvest homes and wedding feasts
And sales of surplus plant and beasts.

And, once, inside the sagging door,
John Wesley's voice was heard to roar,
And men in smocks had fits and cried
And tore their hair as he untied
The ropes that wrapped their rustic life
In bondage, poverty and strife;
And gave them hope that Christ would save
A place for them beyond the grave.

*** John Wesley and Charles, his brother, often visited Donington Hall in
the mid-18th century. John was said to have preached at Park Farm and
Kings Mills. Selina, Countess of Huntingdon, was almost a Calvinist and
built several Non-conformist chapels.*

THE LAKE

At Donington Park

The midges and mosquitos bit
My face and neck so much I lit
A pipe and watched the lake
As rising trout began to take
The may-fly nymphs and moulting dun.
A sullen sky, a sinking sun,
A whispering shook the willow trees
And rushes shivered in the breeze,
And pheasant cocks in rising flight
From ground to roost bade all "goodnight."
The mallard flight came swooping round
And landed with a swishing sound
To preen and squawk. I knew what fun
I could have had with rod and gun;
But was content to be so near
To see the leaping trout and hear
The cocks ascend, and, as the light
Began to fade, to see the flight
Of wild fowl swoop from out the sky.
I never bothered to untie
My rod or take from out the sleeve
My gun, that warm September eve.

THE MASTER BUCK

In Donington Park, Leicestershire

He stays within his rutting ground
And guards it with a belching groan,
He frays the foliage all around
The boundaries of this mating zone.
Beneath each eye a sensual gland
Secretes a scent to stain the twigs
And mark his parkland rutting stand.
The two fore-feet with which he digs
Have scent glands, too, that impregnate
The scrapes he makes to wallow in;
He urinates to irrigate
The soil to plaster on has skin;
And proudly poses in his prime,
The king of all the dappled deer;
His winter coat all caked in slime,
Pugnacious, pungent, void of fear;
New antlers now adorn his head,
Their velvet sheen all scraped away
And, hard of horn, and palms well spread,
He'll clash with the lesser bucks that prey
Upon his patch. His stance and smell
Attract October does to stay
And these he keeps within his spell
And vigilance. He will not stray
To other ground, and neither eats or sleeps.
Within three weeks, all passion spent,
 His duty duly done, he creeps
 Away, worn out, to rest content.

*** There has been a Deer Park at Donington since the 12th century. There
are still There are still over 300 head there now, both Red and fallow.*

In Grandad's Day

At Isley Walton Manor

In Grandad's day, the croquet lawn
Was shaved and flat and green.
To mow and roll, old Bess was used to tow
The staunch machine, her shoes withdrawn,
And in their place were leather pads
Enwrapped around her heavy hooves
That left no trace of equine grooves.
The Gardener, Fred, and his two lads
Were busy here from dawn to dark
With barrow, bucket, rake or spade;
And, when it rained or snowed, they made
Indoors to tend to vines or mark
The pricked-out plants, or pot the pink
Geraniums. The endless trays
Of seeds and bulbs, the ferns and sprays
Of hanging baskets, make me think
Of Babylon as sprinklers played
From pipes above. The peach and palm
And potted plants dispensed a balm
Of tropic scents; and air was made
More pungent with the smell the red
Tomatos gave. I could not dwell
For long inside that hot-house hell
My eyes would swell with tears, my head
Would hurt, I'd sneeze and wheeze. The men
Retired for lunch mid-day inside
The potting shed and I would sit beside
The fire and Fred would tell of when
He was a soldier-boy and fought

The sullen Boers, of Spion Kop
And Mafeking and how to stop
A bleeding wound, and how he caught
The Pox in Ladysmith. I thought
It strange, for I was very young,
That soldier-boys could be so stung
By touching titled ladies; he taught.
Me how to hone my penknife blade
And how to slice, and graft, and bud;
And cut me arrows from the wood
And shaped a bow of yew. He made
A whipping top for me with whip
Of leather thong. They shared with me
Red Leicester cheese and sweet cold tea
And bread and dripping, and a sip
Of parsnip wine. I even tried
To chew tobacco soaked in rum;
(But much preferred my chewing gum).
When my favourite kitten died
They made a cross and buried him
Inside a tin among the mounds
Of many cats and birds and hounds
The family had loved. No trim
And sacred cemetery received
More tender care than this dear plot
Of buried pets. And on this spot
I planted daffodils and grieved
For many days. Sometimes I spent
My boy-hood days with Keeper, Tom,
Who lost a leg upon the Somme,
But Grandad kept him on. He went,
With crutches under arms, around
The woods and nests, and catching pens,
And coops with chicks and bantam hens

That lined the close-cropped rearing ground.
And Jack, his son, would trap and snare;
And 'sifty' John was up all night
To keep the copper kilns alight,
And boil and stir the gruel, and scare
Away the wily fox. The feed
Was mainly eggs and lettuce leaves,
Oat-meal, millets, peas and greaves,
And spinach, rice, and dari seed,
And boiled potatoes, barley-flake,
And kibbled maize, and custard, groats,
And wheat well crushed and onions, oats,
And buck-wheat, beans and biscuit-cake;
And sometimes drops of anti-gape
And feather tonic, liver oil
Would join the steaming gruel to foil
Disease or stunted growth. With cape
And hat like Sherlock Holmes, old Tom
Would stalk his bounds and talk
About the vermin stoat and hawk,
The weasel, raven, rat; and from
His neck there hung a phial
Of poison "fit to kill a county town."
He put a speck inside a brown
Ratskin or eggs, and all the while
I walked behind, he talked of jays
And carrion crows and pole-cat pests
And pine-martins, and pheasant nests
Disturbed by dogs and all the ways
He'd deal with those who steal at night.
He taught me how to hold a gun,
To "Never leave a loaded one",
And what was wrong and what was right,
And "Never act the fool or clown".

The golden rule of his wise school
Was "let your gun be like your tool,
And that is, lad, right up or down!"
The vermin larder was a sight
I never liked to see. I thought
It odd no 'Charlie fox' was bought
To hang on gallows there. "Not right"
Said Tom, "To let a fox be seen
With all those pests". I knew of pens,
A feathered mass of headless hens,
To show where knashing teeth had been
In early hours - A keeper's work
Of many months completely spoiled,
And all his safety measures foiled
By some unwariness or quirk
Or careless or unwitting lapse
Of prudence. Badgers may have grubbed
Up wire in search of wasps or rubbed
The wicket gate; or John, perhaps,
Had dropped asleep. I never knew
Of foxes killed within our grounds
Except those hunted by the hounds
Who never failed to find. A few,
No doubt, were quietly 'put away'
And buried deep without display
In Ramsley Wood or Brick-Yard Clay;
But nothing said that could betray
This secret culling of our prey.
Tom knew my family all rode
To hounds and could not break the code
Of hunting Shires, whereby to slay
In such a way, was Vulpicide,
A crime engendering much hate
In Leicestershire and quite as great

As murder, rape or Regicide!
We children hunted with the Quorn
If not too far away to hack
Our ponies to the meet - and back;
And, if it was a cubbing morn,
We rose at dawn with many a yawn
And off we got to Breedon Cloud
To slap our saddle flaps full loud
To keep the cubs in covers drawn.
We saw the golden sun arise
O'er Donington and stood around
Old Ramsley Wood where deer are found.
We heard the huntsman's rate chastise
The hounds and saw the game birds rise
Like rockets out of the wood and heard
Old Tom declare, as the pheasants whirred
Above his head, "this exercise
Will do 'em good, they learn to fly
At tree-top height for better sport
On main-wood shooting days. There's nought
So bad as low birds, lad, those high
And wild are good!" And when the days
For proper hunting came, we rode
For miles 'at walk' or 'trot' by road
And field and tracks and bridle-ways
And over stiles and timber rails,
(But not yet let our ponies sweat),
To get to meets in time, and set
About the walls and rocky dales.
Of Charnwood. At half past-three we said
"Good night!" and let the girths go slack;
We had to hack our ponies back
Before the day-light went, and fed,
And brushed, and bedded down, with all

The dirty tack well dunked and hung
Before the bath time bell was rung
And supper served at Breedon Hall.
And as we dined we told our tales
Of daring deeds and frightful falls
And how we leapt those fearsome walls
And cantered up those verdant vales.
I dreamt, those nights, of runs that day,
Of ghostly hunts with phantom packs
From hangman's Stone to Battle flats,
From Charnwood Heath to Stewards Hay,
From Whitwick Waste to Maple Well
And Abbot's Oak to Agar's Nook,
To Swanimote and Beacon Brook,
From Peldor Tor on past the shell
Of Ulverscroft's old Abbey Church
To Hammercliff and Breakback Hill,
And up Earls Dyke to Charley Mill,
To Chitterman and cross to search
In Craven's rough. They gave their best
Up Beacon Hill and down the gorse
To hanging Stones and right on course
To end the day at Black-Bird's Nest

1930

** *My grandfather, John Gillies Shields (1857-1943) was an Alderman, J.P, C.C and farmer. Born in Scotland he became Agent to the Earl of Loudoun and Baron Donington. He eventually bought the Donington Estate. His eldest son, my father (Major Johnny) captained Leicestershire C.C.C and played for the Gentlemen of England.*

SONG OF DESPAIR

Felixstowe

Wind whips the water front and whines
In wires above. The waves rebound
And spray descends: The night eye shines
With drunken winks from buoys that round
The bay are reeling. Lashing rain
Is pounding cheeks already wet
With tears that tell of desperate pain
Within my heart that can't forget
It's shame. Will these dark seas release
The chain and let me float in peace?
And will they drown the brow's sad crease
And cause all pain and anguish cease
And wash away all yesterday
To purify the past? And will
They nullify my mind and stay
My sleep narcotically and still
The tortured breast ? Can they but seal
Up sadness, smother hate and yet
Not kill my hopes complete or steal
My doubting soul! - To slide and let
The sleep of deep lull life away
In streams dispelling all unrest
That take the spirit to the bay
Of dreams and there to re-invest
It's being! Wake me on the shore
Of virgin sand, to breath again
The sweetest air, to live once more
In child-like innocence! "In vain
You Die!" the seagulls cry, "No heart

Can beat upon the land that's been
Asleep below: no one can part
The sea-weed chains that bind the green
And grotesque graves that groan
In ocean beds. Only the brave
Deserve what they desire and own
The key to second birth and save
Their souls; For cowards are not born
Again; so turn meekly and seek
Repentance, facing doubt with scorn".
They circle round the rocky creek
And shriek defiance at the sea.
I hesitate, then hear above
Their voices crying down to me,
"Go back young man, and prove your love!
There is no answer deep below
But black oblivion, Go home!
Go home! All will be well, we know!"
I heard the hungry oceans' endless strife,
And knew that gulls with angels play
And wings were wishing back my life
From death deep in the boiling bay.

1947

THE WEATHER WAR

Felixstowe

All the water front was weeping
With the wounds received in keeping
Surging seas from leaping
From the shore.

And the world of man was sleeping
While the waves to war were creeping
Bent on inland sweeping,
Evermore.

Spiteful clouds above were spitting
Cover fire and thunder, splitting
Skies asunder, hitting
Hard the foe.

Weather-witches helped by sitting,
Stitching sheets of sleet and knitting
Rolls of fog for gripping
Earth below.

Concrete cracked and quays were quaking
Proud, prim, promenades were shaking,
Monstrous waves were breaking
O'er the pier.

Sea Knights fell in cascades making
Mounted white horse charges, taking
On the ramparts aching
With the wear.

Like Bath Tub Toys
The dripping Buoys were slipping low,
Skippimg high and bobbing here,
Tipping there, as in a hurricane.

Wires were whining with the whipping
Welted out by wind and ripping
Canvas flapped as shipping
Took the strain.

Trying to shelter from the thrashing,
Piles of pebbles panicked clashing
Pelter-welter, dashing
Up the beach.

High on land the foam was crashing,
Splashing over dome and slashing
Flashy booths and smashing
All in reach

Peace comes with an Eastern glowing
From the sun that's slowly growing,
Melting clouds and slowing
Down the storm.

Crowing witches ceased their sewing
Knowing that as heat comes flowing,
All their powers were going
With the warm.

Deep now beats retreat with swilling
Rearguard madly milling, willing
To renew the killing
At sun wane.

Soon the human world is spilling
From the towns and slowly filling
No man's sands and grilling
Midst the slain.

COUNTRY GIRL

Janet

I love your slightly twisted nose,
Your wispy straw-gold hair;
I love your casual country clothes,
The silly hats you wear.
Your eyes are blue as summer skies
As tenderly they seek
For beauties truth. I love the sighs
That seep from breasts and speak
The secrets of the heart and say
What speech denies; And oh!
I love those parted lips that play
Such games which leave me so,
Well, underdone! I love those small
Reluctant domes, your waist
And bony hips; and that's not all,
I love the time you waste
On such a clumsy clown as I.
I love you for your ways
Of grace that seem to make all my
Mid-age, September days.

Song for the City Man

Poor man, perhaps you've never heard
The joyous cry of wakening bird,
Nor seen the sun rise from its bed
Or sink inside its blanket red.
You've never paused to watch, in streams,
The gliding fish, or parted beams
Of sunlight speckled dust through glass;
Or naked walked the dewy grass
Before the moon has sighed away
Another night watch over day.
No doubt you've missed the smell of smoke
From burning leaves that kiss and soak
The autumn air, nor heard the peals
As Sunday bells bring God to fields
And ring around echoing hills:
For these are things to cure your ills;
The cuckoo's call in early May,
The sweetness of the new mown hay
The patterns on the frozen pane,
The harvest mouse on golden grain.
The bowing trees before the gale,
The taste of milk direct from pail,
The beauty of the flowering thorn,
The sprouting, hedge, the lambs newborn.
The soft warm glow of candle light,
The flickering flames of logs by night;
The lark from clover, rising high,
The drumming snipe, the curlew cry;
And have you ever listened to
The courting woodie's coo, coo, coo?

The rising trout, the salmons leap,
A baby in his cot asleep,
The elegance of dry stone walls
The wheels of mills and water falls,
The water from a mountain spring
The morning chorus that birds sing.
There are so many things to see,
And smell, and hear, and all are free
And ever fresh. Your gold and deals
Your power and paunch, your pills at meals,
Your sleeping draughts and drugs, and hairs
That whiten every hour; your fears
And files and frantic rush in town
Put years upon your days and crown
Your life, when last retirement comes,
With ulcers, aches and toothless gums.
O take a holiday! - no scene
Of southern seas, no cruising Queen,
No planes or trains -just peal off pride
And ride and walk the country-side.

For You Alone, Ann

Song

*I*n spring the birds are singing
From lark to turtle-dove,
And bells are blissfully swinging
In steeples high above
These songs and peals are ringing
For you alone, my love.

With July comes romancing
For flowers in summer clothes
With mellow scents entrancing
The magic of rainbows.
All these are gaily dancing
To please you, alone, my rose.

The golden leaves are falling,
The air is crisp and clear
As autumn comes in crawling,
I hear the rutting deer;
And pheasant cocks are calling
As I call you, my dear.

When winter winds are blowing
The creaking rafters groan,
And fields are white with snowing
And frosts freeze to the bone;
My logs are brightly glowing
For you, alone, my own.

A RONDEL

Elizabeth

With trembling hands I carved a heart
Upon a weeping willow tree
And then, for all the birds to see,
I pierced it with a cupid's dart;
I wrote beneath this rustic art
A passion-blending 'G. loves E.'
With trembling hands I carved a heart
Upon a weeping willow tree.

You came upon me with a start,
Then, blushing sweetly, said to me
"Elizabeth loves you" and we
Became impossible to part!
With trembling hands I carved a heart
Upon a weeping willow tree.

THE HAND THAT HOLDS THE PEN

The hand that holds the pen can crush
The rose or plunge the knife or place
The poison pill; or wield a brush
To limn a dream or subtly trace
The tremors of our hearts. So long
Ago it seems, that day of skies
Alive with curlew cries, the song
Of soaring larks and wistful sighs
And moistened eyes and whispered words
That lit our lips with love. That day
We lay in scented hay the birds
Had reason to be gay and play
At Cupid's's game When hearts unite
And darts abound, the sparks of love
Are spread around to set alight
Our hearts, while skylarks sing above
Contented cows at grass
Around our nesting bed. I felt
The flesh force through your glove and pass
Its message to my mind and melt
The bars I live behind and call
Convention to unwind and give
Our love release. But this was all
So long ago and now we live
With wasted years of doubts and fears,
And miles of love-locked land between
That hand and mine. If smiles to tears
Have turned - my love is ever green,
Upon the rope of hope I lope
Above the brink of death, and sink

And rise from post to post and grope
With desperate need to grab the link
That's left, the envelope which seals
Inside the waves of hope that drown
The pain within my breast breast and heals
The brain-cells' ache, and tells the frown
On furrowed brow to rest at peace.
With every letter that you send
You grace it with a kiss to cease
The strife inside my mind and mend
Suspicions sorry sore. You write,
And when I read, I feel the glow
Inside my soul, and see the light
Of tearful eyes illume the slow
Quixotic smile you gave and sense
The silken tongues' soft tones bestow,
A honeyed balm to calm my tense
Despair and melt the flow of snow
And free my frozen mind. I need
Your news, the lungs of love, the food
To feed an addict's greed, the deed
Of mercy and the sanctitude
Of sanity. The hand that holds
The pen injects the insulin
Of ink and when the page unfolds
I feel, once more, a paladin
Arrayed for knightly quest. The hand
That holds the pen can grip
The knife and cut the mooring strand
And let the ship of love just slip
Astray from land and drift and float
In aimless tides of grief. I pray
Your hand may make secure my boat
To bollards deep in earth away

From shifting sands of change beside
Your berth inside the sheltered bay:
And evermore, to moor or glid;
Upon the rippling tide. We'll stay
Together, side by side, and keep
As loyal as royal swans and weigh
Our anchors chain to chain till sleep
Descends to gently rock and sway
Us in our cradles o the sea.
The hand that holds the pen can take
The key and turn the lock and free
The refugee of fear and break
The chains of doubt and heal the poor
Neglected wounds within; Or this
Same hand can lock the dreaded door,
Ignore the knock and shout, dismiss
The tears that blind, and ties that bind
A lover's knot, and block the ears
To seal all sounds that hurt the mind
And stop the clock our future wears.
I crave once more, I beg, implore,
You let me have your hand again
And feel its vein of love restore
My peace from pain and help regain
Those happy halcyon days and close
The doors of doubt. And so to end
This plea. I humbly now enclose
A ring - a simple thing, to send
A friend - but there's a special band
Of magic hair entwined within
This precious band of gold - a wand
Of virgin strands that fairies spin
To bring a cure to fears of old
To mend the rift between we two

And dry the tears of time and hold
Us bound for evermore with true
And pure unfettered love. This gift,
With all I haveI send, and live
Until you bringit back and lift
A finger bathed in gold and give
The hand that held the pen for me
To hold and feel our pulses blend
Into a fusion bound to be
As one until our very end.

THE ROSE

Seraglios
Of infidels,
And Porticos
Of southern belles,
Divine grottoes
And muscatels,
Around them grows
The rose!

Of Shinar's woes
Of Sharon's wells,
Of damask hose,
Of philomels.
Of Jericho's
Old citadels
Of such echoes
The rose.

When in the throes
Of love's sweet hells,
When beaux propose
To demoiselles,
When in the rows
Of stage door swells,
Bouquets compose
Of rose

From all the clothes
Flora expels
In petal blows
To elfin dells
Like pinks jocose
And asphodels;
The fairies chose
The rose.

The blind man's nose
With wonder tells
Of indigos
And muscatels,
Damson pear and sloes
And orchard smells,
0! what he owes
The rose!

The garden throws
It's carousels
With boleros
For immortelles
And fandangos
For pimpernels;
But flamencos
For rose.

Mullatto's pose
Like shy gazelles
In calico's
And beads of shells,
With hair that flows
With magic spells
And halo glows
Of rose.

With satin bows
A girl excels
With scarlet toes
And bottled smells,
Yet none of those
Will ring the bells
Unless she shows
The rose.

When quarrels close
Where friendship dwells,
The peace to foes,
The gift that tells
Of love that grows;
The wreaths farewells
With all these goes,
The rose.

DEAR ROSE, A SONG

A song to someone who was very ill.

Upon the garden of my heart there grows
A radiant rose; nor fades the smell
Of scented dew that all around her flows;
By day the petals gaily tell
Of love that overflows; at dusk they close
With silent sighs into the shell
Of sleep. So like this rose is her repose,
So moist her petalled eyes! How well
Upon her tranquil face the moonshine glows
With mystic grace and casts its spell
Upon my cell of beating breath. Who knows
When God may transpose her to dwell
In His own garden dell ? But if she goes
Nothing shall quell my breath's farewell;
For I will die with my dear rose.

MARKING TIME

All worldly ties I sever,
The towel is thrown,
I stay alone,
Forsaking all endeavour.
No forward move
From out this groove
Withdrawing backwards, never.
No halt until
My heart is still,
I'm marking time forever.

Your kiss was like a feather
That floats on air;
Your lips a snare
That ties me to a tether.
A poisoned dart
Has pierced my heart
And turned its love to leather.
Your fickle fire
Has burnt desire,
Destroyed our life together.

MILL GIRLS

The Mill has closed. It was the pride
Of all the town. No-one to blame.
Its usefulness wore out and died.
A way of life has gone and shame
And anguish fill the hearts of all
Who laboured there from in their teens
To when they wore the Granny shawl,
And are now rejects and has-beens.
The 'phone cut off. The car now stays
Unused inside the port. All goods on hire
Have been returned and holidays
Are wishful dreams. The fates conspire
When one is down to keep one there
And heap calamities on blight.
Depression, boredom and despair
Unhinge the home, and envy, spite
And jealousy can slowly seep
Into the vacuum left by love.
Entitlements can only keep
Afflicted families above
The begging bowl. They cannot cope
With idleness and empty days
With pride and dignity and hope,
And muggers in the alley ways.
The centre of town is dead,
The Chapel is a bingo hall.
And parents fear as pushers spread
Their evil nets at night and trawl
For children's lives. And petty crime
Increases with the need to buy
The drugs. The club, that overtime
Had kept alive, will slowly die.

The pub and pawn shop will thrive too well
As many shops shut down. The old
Alone still heed the Sunday bell;
As though the church has lost its hold
On people's lives just when they need
It most. The trendy Vicar tries
His best. He comes from that new breed
Of Pinkish Priests whose stance implies
A compromise with Marx. The bright
New school in spacious fields should fill
The dullest child with hope and light
The way, for children of the Mill,
To better skills, is now a store
Of discontent where discipline
And pride departed through the door
When teachers went on strike to win
More pay. Politicians beat
Their breasts with pious platitudes
And promise things to keep their seat;
The Union Leaders' attitudes
Are still embedded in the past
With Luddite overtones.
They call for strikes that cannot last
And hit their heads against the wall
Of cold indifference. The works
Now closed were started by one man.
A dormant latent talent lurks
In every gifted artisan.
As acorns into oaks can grow
So seeds of enterprise can yield
A crop of industry. To sow
The grains of hope upon this field
Of fallow weeds, there must be found
Creative brains to drive the drill

And scatter seeds on willing ground.
The wheel has turned. The worn out Mill
Is dead. Do not despair; but think
Of when it was not there and how
A man of vision did not shrink
From taking risks; but set his plough
In virgin soil. Recall that man
And how his enterprise began !

THE MAZE OF LOVE

I often wonder why you stand
So silent by the window sill,
And see, in far off fields, a land
That never was and never will
Be walked by you. And with sad eyes
You scan the skies for some true sign
Of hope, and sift the stars with sighs
At night for one more clue divine
That might unwind the ropes that bind
Your soul with knots so tight. If pride
Was pruned and forced to fall behind
Less selfish vines, the hurts you hide
Inside might heal, and from the roots
Would rise a richer food to feed
Your mind with sweeter, softer, shoots.
And then, I think, you'd feel the need
To air your sorrows in the sun:
And if the glare was too severe,
I'd share my shade with you, and one
By one, your cares would disappear.
Your heart has crawled inside a shell,
And cannot feel the tears that fall
Or hear my prayers. That private hell
Of yours can hold no cures, for all
The germs of fear increase in heat
And darkness there, and canker creeps
More deep. Grim visions you secrete
In some forbidden safe that keeps
Them in a frozen sleep. The key,

You say, you tossed away, and lost.
O let me help you look and free
The door, and thaw, behind, the frost,
And cure the blindness of your mind!
You wander strange unearthly ways
And roam up secret rides: You wind
Around a moonbeam land, a maze
Of silvery haze, and gaze at flowers
Who seem to sigh and shake their heads
As you go by. You lean long hours
Upon the bridge and watch the threads
Of life float on, and dream, and wish,
And wonder why you cannot keep
Up with the stream just like the fish
That gleam and glide below. You sleep
No deep relaxing rest; but lay
Your head upon a bed of thorn
And wake more weary with each day
Which makes you look and feel forlorn.
These wanderings will never come
To ought but deadly ends - for sad
Unhappy souls. The total sum
Of all your ponderings will add
To nought. Desires and yearnings creep
Upon your dreams to cry protest
At schemes you've put aside. They keep
Out sleep who longs to be your guest
And gnaw and nag till nerves are raw
And ragged with their work. O, live
With me and lie with me; Withdraw
From out your shell! Each night I'll give
My heart to you and wrap it round

Your own, and in the morn you'll wake
 Refreshed from sleep that's only found
Within a lover's arms. I'll make
You live again and laugh again
And wipe away the rears ans strife
And soothe the seething in your brain
And lull you slowly back to life.

DEBBIE J.

Outside the church, that wedding day,
You looked so lovely that, despite
My advanced age and hair of grey,
I felt the warmth of love delight
My weary heart, and seem to stay
Within and warmer get that night,
On Repton's lawn. To my dismay,
Inside the hall, I lost all sight
Of you and made to sit away
With clever dicks; I got quite tight
On good red wine to drown the way
I felt. I could not face the flight
Of steps which down I fell and may
Be lamed for life. And so I write
This verse to say to Debbie J,
I love you, dear, in my way, your knight
I am, there is no more to say.

BELIEF 1950

Belief is like a mountain rill
That grows the more it flows downhill;
And man alone can tame its force,
Pollute its goodness, change its course.
He can restrain its strength to make
A reservoir or dam or fishing lake
Or drive it underground. Yet still
The water flows; and man can kill
A man or beast but cannot blow
The wind away or stop the snow
Or clouds or rain or tides, nor can
He kill a mountain rill or ban
Belief for good. The cynics say
All men succumb to gold, betray
Their principles and sell their souls
To save their skins. Yet names on scrolls
Of saints and martyred men would fill
A hundred thousand books and still
Not mention all who gave their life
To keep belief alive. In strife
Between beliefs a million more
Have died; and prisoners by the score
Reside in jails today because
Their conscience clashed with unjust laws.
In grim gulags and labour camps
The springs of faith are damned, and lamps
Of hope are dim; yet here is found
The bleeding Christ, the breeding ground
Of faith, the joy of Allah, the beam
In Buddha's eye, the constant gleam
Of New Jerusalem. To feed
His soul a man must have a creed,

A need to serve, worship and pray,
To thank, to love and to obey.
Belief in God surpasses all
Beliefs of other kinds that call
For sacrifice, like beliefs
In tribal lands or tribal chiefs,
In monarchs, Marx, dictators' dreams.
Its right these ancient ardent streams
Of secular beliefs should flow
Within their legal bounds and owe
Allegiance to their springs of birth.
If foreign torrents swamp their earth,
Invade their waterways, the strife
Will last as long as human life,
As seen today in many lands,
From Palestine to Chaddean sands,
From Cyprus, Ulster, Amazon,
From Baltic states to Lebanon,
From Burma to Afghanistan,
Tibetan hills to Kurdistan.
As bigots and the zealots rail
And bomb and kidnap for blackmail
Its hard for Gods above to know
The terrorists from those that show
The freedom flag. The water wheel
Of time evolves to slowly heal
The wounds of hate. Let paddles churn
For compromise, with purpose turn
For tolerance, humility, goodwill
And common sense so peace can spill
From out the mill and hate and pride
And ignorance be cast aside.

HYMN

Show me, Lord the road,
Keep me near thy side,
Lighten, Lord, my load,
Lest I downward slide.

Lessen, Lord, my pains,
Humble, Lord, my pride;
Loosen, Lord, my chains,
Lead on, Lord, my guide.

Through the vale of tears
Heavenwards, uphill,
Banish all my fears,
Strengthen, Lord, my will.

Strip me, Lord, of greed,
Clean the stains of years,
Save me, Lord, I plead;
 Hearken to my prayers.

THE VISITOR

*A dream, following the visit of the Archbishop of
Canterbury to the Pope in Rome*

There was no message in His face
To spell out colour, class or race
Or lines to tell of time. His eyes
Were harbours choked with ships of sighs
Awash with all the tears of years
Of human cries and prayers and fears.
He wore the clothes a man might wear
Away from bench or field or chair;
He bore no banner, wore no card,
As he approached the palace yard.
He paused beside the mitred gate
And pulled the bell of church and State.
"The hour is late," the Curate said
"My Lord and staff are all abed,
So state your case and quickly go!"
But as he spoke, a mystic glow
Of golden light appeared to melt
The gloom of night. The Curate felt
And saw, and knelt upon the floor
Before the stranger at the door.
"I did not know, I did not know"
He deeply sobbed and bent so low
As though to kiss the feel that bled
A thousand years ago. His head
Was gently lifted up. "Arise
My friend! My time is short, the cries
Of China Call and over all
The East there looms the ugly pall

Of poverty, so close to hell.
Just tell his Grace my prayers will dwell
Upon his fight to help unite
The Christian world and set alight
The fire of faith, igniting dead,
Deserted, hope, whose sparks will spread
To kindle peace and warm the wine
Of love and bake the bread divine.
The human race may conquer space
Yet leave it's soul behind, and race
To planets, pure of sin, to flood
Their virgin springs with poisoned blood;
And taint the air and paint with fear
The atmosphere of stars – yet veer
Away from God. No resting place,
No peace, tranquility and grace
Awaits material man until
He works on earth the ways and will
Our father has in heaven. Tell
The Bishop that he pleases well;
For all the angels start to sing
When hearing shepherds call to bring
Their wayward flocks back to the fold
Of God; to slay the wolves of old
Dissents and feed the need of hope
To long divided groups that grope
In dark and danger-ridden ways.
Before one cross the Christian prays;
Yet different dogmas, rituals, creeds
Have blinded leaders to the needs
Of God alive this day. His Grace
Has wielded well his shepherd's mace
And helped to heal the broken home
By holding out his hand to Rome,

And tried to seal the running sore
That saps the cross's strength before
The jeers of evil men in red
Who rule with fear where faith is dead.
And with those words he faded back
Into the bosom of the black
Unconscious night. The Curate woke
And saw the solid room, the oak
Unchanged, his bed, substantial things,
And knew his dream had come on wings
As in the wilderness to John
To wake, to warn and act upon.
He opened up his window wide
And heard the hungry lambs outside
And smelt the blossom scented breeze
That floated from the singing trees,
And heard from every earthy sound
The God of Love had been around.

DE PROFUNDIS

Do weep for me when I have gone
To meet the maker of my soul.
It's right to mourn when men pass on
And let the tears of sorrow roll
Unchecked down cheeks. For life is born
In pain to stay its course then fades
The way of flowers. You should not scorn
The need to grieve or spurn the aids
Of sympathy. Let change be slow.
The bond of Love outlives one's breath
And stays in memory's store to show
Its power is deeper far than death
And can't be cast aside as waste
For garbage men to glean. Its wrong
To change the old routine in haste,
The habits that we knew so long,
The sounds and smells and scenes and sights
We shared. And when I'm dead you're bound
To dread the loneliness of nights,
The empty bed, and, sobbing, pound
The pillows with your fists until
You feel my presence there and slide
Away to sleep, My spirit will
Absorb the shocks of death and guide
You through distress, its power recedes
As time diminishes its need.
Its right to wear the widow's weeds
And heed the mourning wake and lead
The family we raised with pride
And dignity to my grave-side;
Then drink a toast to one who tried

To limn poetic lines, and died.
And when alone at Eventide
Its right to cry at things you see
Around the rooms and sigh beside
My rocking chair and think of me.
When silence smoothes the brow of day
And night draws down her blind,
The house may still have things to say
To deep recesses in your mind.
Do not despair then, if you hear
Nocturnal esoteric strains
The house may whisper in your ear;
Or thunderstorms and bitter rains
May shake the fabric in protest;
The wind may wail in attic eaves
And rake the red-brick chimney breast
And fill the gutters full of leaves
So water pours down window panes
And falls down walls in sheets and clogs
The gurgling pipes and swirling drains.
The fire may squeal with sodden logs
And shutters beat like kettle drums
That pulsate to the purl of wires
Outside, as wind upon them strums
The melodies of ancient lyres.
No doubt, old Sheeba, faithful hound,
Will place his head on paws and whine
Beside my bed for master gone to ground.
Its right to let the old dog pine
And comfort him the best you can.
And both of you may hear with fear
A creaking chair as though a man
Is rocking there, and other queer
Disturbing sounds, the cistern sings,

A vixen screams and, from the thatch,
A barn-owl hoots and flaps his wings;
A squeaking hinge, a lifted latch,
A doorknob turns, a rush of air,
A floor board groans and seems to say
That someone's' standing on the stair.
But all these fears will fade away
As mourning dues are paid in tears.
And you must gather up the reins
And leave the ashes of burnt years,
Our pyre of past desires and pains,
And ride from Winter into Spring
To face whatever fate may bring.

Classroom Clay, 1946

On being asked to subscribe to a school memorial.

The soil of England lies so rich for therein lives the blood
Of all our greatness and the seeds which ripen into youth.
The bones remain to fertilize the flowers which hold the bud
Of knowledge, bloom of beauty, and the greenest leaves of truth
That only grow on English soil so long as those who live
Deserve its grace. For should the Nation rot with greed, decay
Like Rome of old, then shall the soil reveal its shame and give
But weed from seeds. The buried dead become the classroom clay
That's mixed and moulded, shaped and smoothed upon the desks of schools;
Here come the boys, as unpolluted clay, so soft, so clean
So fresh from flowering river banks of English life; No tools
Are used to frame their shape, no heartless pattern punch machine,
Or hammer knocks their heads about to regiment their brains,
No file employed to smooth off points of individual trait;
But strong, unselfish, hands with wisdom running rich through veins
Create the future's fertile minds for managing the state;
As pride, corruption, lust and power destroyed the soul of Greece,
O England let not poison stain your streams! O watch your seed!
Keep clean your banks, husband the flowers that pollinate with peace
The fields of other lands. Mourn not the dead, they live and bleed
And need no statues empty stare or fading wreathes put by.
Give thanks with bright perpetual blooms and plough the land with skill,
And those whose bones lie low abroad will know they did not die,
But left behind a richer soil for all to love and till.

Ditilawa, Ceylon

Recovering, from Malaria

The moon, a silver magnet, drew
Me from my dreams,
And down the night I wandered through
Its silent beams.
I strode the silver streets until
The end of town,
And slowly started up the hill
And there sat down
Beneath a sky of eastern stars;
And heard the thrum
Of distant drum and sad sitars
And sweet, the hum
Of softly singing Sinhalese.
I heard the groan
From far away, the wail, the wheeze,
The gasps, the moan
Of anguish, squeals of wheels in pain
As round the bends
The train from Kandy feels the strain
As it ascends
The hill. The scavengers of dark
Perform their rights,
And snarling pariah dogs that bark
In greedy fights
For carrion from a panther's kill,
And keep at bay
The slobbering jackals that mill
Around and bray
Their insane laughter to the night.

I heard, far-off,
The wild hog snort in startled fright,
A leopard's cough,
And then the screech owl's eerie scream,
And saw the eyes
Of chital deer in moon light gleam;
And heard the cries
Of jungle cocks disturbed from sleep
By lantern flairs
As native trappers gently creep
To lay their snares
The trees were bright with fire-fly lights
And gliding packs
Of flying foxes flew in flights
Like vampire bats
To feed on fruit. The croaking crake
The tree frog made
Combined with those cicardas make
In forest glade
Pulsated through the air a sound
Of rhythmic throbs.
And boughs began to shake all round
As angry mobs
Of monkeys screamed as one lone bear
In search of bees
Began to prowl and growl too near
Their bed-time trees.
A mongoose hunted near
My feet and tried
To open up my pack and peer
Inside, then spied
My face and stared at me with eyes
So feared by snakes.
He bounded off with peevish cries

Towards the lakes
Below. And I lay back and felt
At peace and sighed
For war to cease. With joy I smelt
On every side
The smells and spells and scents of trees,
The flame-tree's flower,
The fragrant frangipanis
Majestic power.
An old bull elephant trumped aloud,
A bugle blew;
The sky became a cloak of cloud,
As wind lashed through
.The tall bamboo and rain began
To fall, and ants
Invaded all my clothes and ran
Inside my pants.
The midges stung, mosquitos bit
My neck and head,
My seat became a watery pit
And leeches bled
My arms and legs. I rose to leave
My forest hide
And with sadness began to weave
And slip and slide
My way below. My heart remained
With all the charms.
Of Ceylon's paradise. I'd gained,
In Lanka's arms.
The peace that calms a soldier's breast
Where ever ship
May take me now, my heart will rest
In Serendip.

AFRICAN NIGHTS

Oh! African nights I have known!
And the cries of the land I have heard,
Like the growl of a lion on a lone
Hungry prowl and the hooves of the herd
On the run. And the gnashing of bone
By a corpse, and the cubs as they purred
With the fill of a kill. And the moan
Of the calves in the Kraals as they're stirred
By a leopard that crawls round the stone
Rubble walls; and the strange anvil bird
With its haunting refrain and the drone
Of the drums of the dancers who whirred
With their songs of monotonous tone.

1940

African nights I have known,
Sounds of the Veldt I have heard,
Howls of a lion on his lone
Furtive patrol near a herd
Crossing the land that he owns;
Cubs at a kill, gnashing of bones,
Growlings and contented moans.
And from the side of the round
Palisades, prickly with thorn,
Girding all stock safe and sound
From the sun going down 'til dawn,
Came the dry cough of a proud

Leopardess prowling too near,
Causing the goats to bleat loud,
While the long horn cows, in fear,
Snortled and pawed at the ground.
Beating tin cans, little guard
Boys awoke all the compound
Tribesmen to arms. The bombard
Soon began, curses profane
Noising the night for an hour.
Murmuring too, from the plain,
Came from the game on the scour
For scanty grass near the lake
Where elephants bathed and blew
Watery trumpets at day-break.
Bellowing buffalo, too,
Made themselves heard. I have known
Wonderful drums in the night
Each with its different tone
Giving me joy and delight
In hearing dazed dances sing
Jubilant songs. Yes, I fell
For the thrum of the pulsating
Drum and cling to that spell
Whatever else life may bring
Or wherever I may dwell.

SENTRY AT NIGHT

Note: Some young town-bred soldiers were sometimes awfully afraid of
night sentry duty on Historic or Religious sites.
For more information on ghostly sightings or phantom Hosts seen in the
sky, Eldrich scenes, see *Enchanted Britain* by Marc Alexander 1981.
Book Club Associates, London.

Raby Moor - An Eldrich Eve

As you stand all alone in the moon's magic light
When the lone vixen howls and the owl is in flight
And the fallow buck groans, are you shaking with fright
At the noises of night and perceive mystic things?
As when hares on the heath cut displays in great rings,
Or the queen of the witches, with dark spiky wings,
Chases bats from the barn on the back off her broom.
In the empty old church creeps a prophet of doom
Who has prized off the top of his premature tomb,
And is wailing and weeping, his soul in torment,
And the werewolves are howling like hounds on the scent,
At the demons that dance on top of your tent.
In the sacred surrounds of the monastery grounds
Under moss coated stones and the ancient green mounds
Telling tales of man's glory and greed, sacred sounds
Can be heard of the murmuring monks. Holy bones
In their cells cannot cry; but the low dulcet drones
Of their souls soar up in monotonous tones:
As they chant out their plain-song refrain to the air,
Do you hear? do you hear? In their utter despair
Is a call for us all to atone, and to share
In their prayers for the pains of the past when Dane
Came with sword and a king, to the shame of his reign,
With his clerks and their beads, to compute his foul gain.

As the music recedes, do you see a strange sight
Up above? for across the bright stars comes a white
Speckled shroud which is whirling and curling despite
The still air and the whole of the moon - silver sky
Without cloud, but the shapes that you see signify
A re-enactment of war that was fought on this high
Marshy moor many centuries before - on this night;
And the sights that unfold recreate the old fight
With the clans of Scots on this ground. And the light
In the sky is the flashing of steel on chain
And the shields and the armour of knights. And the rain
Is the flights of arrows and spears, and the stain
That is streaking this misty war scene which is spread
On the ceiling of earth, is from wounds that have bled
On these moors; and the pastures are purple and red
Runs the stream as it pours down the valley of blood;
For the flowers of the forest flow down with the flood,
And the pride of the shires lie dead in the mud.
Of these deeds that you see, not a sound can you hear
Of the thrum of the drum, or the horn ringing clear,
Or the clash of claymores, or the plaintive sad air
Of the pibroch's lament for the skeins of wild cocks
Who had flown from their glens, and their mountains and lochs
To a death in the moonlight of moor land and rocks.
As the transient vapours of war disappears
Like the end of a frightening dream, all the fears
Linger long as the grim visage dims in the spheres;
And the plumes on the helmets grow distant and grey,
And the fumes of the fury and the flags fade away;
As the armies withdraw from this Eldritch affray
All to vanish in vapours of translucent steam
And to leave one let down like the end of a dream
Without end or recall. Now the stars are a-gleam
And the moon is supreme and the owl hoots again,

And the badger is rooting for wasp nests and grain
And is turning up bones of an ancient campaign.
And the fox is out ratting in drains around the fold
And is scratching out skulls that are crusty and old
That have lain on these moors, so the story is told,
For two hundred odd years; and they say that at night
In the cold winter time, you can see in the bright
Starry sky the mirage of a war as the white
Spectral hosts in the silent night fight.

1940

REFUGEES - 1945

Displaced Persons Camps in Germany

Like captive creatures in a cage
They stare with sullen eyes;
Or stalk the bounds with silent rage
And rend the air with sighs.
They think of homes and favourite chairs,
Of clocks and cherry trees,
Of tuneful times at country fairs,
And wines and birthday sprees.
In dreams they hear the sound of feet
Upon the pavements of their past
And curse the boots that pound the street
From which they've been outcast.
Creative minds are slowly killed
With endless idle days,
And dead are hands that once were skilled
In countless fruitful ways.
Those statues in the farmers' fields,
Odd scarecrows stuffed with straw,
Do guard, at least, the precious yields
And keep the crows in awe:
But in the camp these creatures seem
To have no task at all
And just like scarecrows in a dream
Around the lager crawl.
The older inmates gave their health
In order to be free,
Will then the West, with all its wealth,
Deny them sanctuary?
For all of us must share the blame

When starving children die
Upon these dunghills of our shame
That rot beneath the sky.
Oh God, please lend your loving light
To help all the kindly lamps
To lead the way to end the plight
Of homeless in the camps.

1947

Note

In 1956 Gillies Shields who had seen D.P. Camps in Germany in 1946 let Donington Hall Rent & Rate free to Refugees run for the Ockenden Venture for 14 years. These included Hungarians, Polish, Latvians and other Balts.
He also worked with other volunteers at the Hall, teaching English and other subjects.

CEYLON

Rubber and tea plantations tamed out of the jungle.

In the Cingalese jungle I've seen
Fighting cocks at their courting displays;
And the shy spotted deer are serene
In a glade, and an elephant sways
In the shade. On the surf, I have been
Under palms round the blueness of bays
With the pools bathed in aquamarine.
And the strumming drum plays as the rays
Of the sun start to peep in between
The parade of the trees as the days
Come alive with the bleeding of lean
Rubber trunks or the taking of trays
In the maze of tea-sprays of green.

1943

SOMALI - 1941

Somali nights were fresh and cool
With dusty winds. I heard the cow
And camel bells tinkling to pool
And pasture ground and thought of how
The land of sand and land of snow
Unite with bells. On Norway hill,
A year ago, I heard the flow
Of ding-a-dell float down and spill
Upon the valley floor. And cows
In Alpine haunts meander meek
And fat to music while they browse
On grasses greenly rich and sweet.
Those bells proclaimed of joyous ease
Of lazy life in healthy air,
Free from drought and dread disease
That falls upon these pastures bare;
Or heat and fear of lion that roam
This dry eroded scrub. No streams
Or stables, stacks of hay or home
Each night for sleep on straw to dreams
Of swedes, await these herds. From wells
To muddy water holes they trek
Across Somali bush, and bells
That hang and clang on every neck
Do toll for life tenacious; tell
Of wearing toil beneath the skies
That blister even tears, and knell
For death in many forms that lies
Along the way. The tick birds pick
At itching backs and vultures claw
At bones, and children's eyes are thick
With flies and legs are lean and raw

With sores. But song and laughter fill
The air, and happy smiles display
Contentment with their lot. The will
Of Allah rules their lives: their day
Is bounded by the sun and all
Their worldly wealth walks with them-wives
And herds. On camels they install
All household goods and frailer lives
- the old and new born babes and bags
Of bladders from the well. And woe
Betide the sickly beast that lags
Behind the trail - for he will go
For meat and skin for clothes. A man
With many wives and cows is great,
And rides up high within the clan;
Accursed the man without - they rate
As useless as an empty well.
With bangles bouncing as they glide
Bedecked in beads of cowrie shell
The women walk with regal pride
That would not shame a Sheba's Queen.
Their breasts are gleaming bronze and bare,
Too beautiful to hide unseen,
And shaped to make the young men stare;
And hips can talk as well as lips
When girls begin to feel inside
The flowers unfurl as cupid nips
Their hearts with darts aimed at a bride.

1941

*J.G.S. had served in Norway in April 1940, returning to U.K. August
1940 after adventures via Sweden and Finland. He served in the
Somaliland Campaign and in Abyssinia, Burma and Germany.*

Nagaland, Burma 1944

Oh, what wonders I saw in the train
Of a war with the troops of the sly
Japanese! And so brave and yet vain
Were the Nagas who reign in their high
Misty hives of their tiger terrain.
With their head-hunting skills they would fly
From the hills to the valley and plain
Far below, and would ambush the dry
River Chong from the curtains of cane;
And with arrows and spears would defy
Modern arms and then melt back again
With the sword of a proud Samurai,
Or the heads of his men they had slain.
They would hunt as if hounds and apply
The sly craft of their primeval brain
Forlaying an ambush and to spy
Every move in their leafy domain.
They could stalk like a cat and cry
All the calls of the wild, the refrain
Of the peacocks and hens and the shy
Sambar deer, and the cough of the bane
Clouded leopard and the grunts of the pie
Coated tapir and hog. They could feign
Such disguise as to blend like a dye
With the greens of the forest and grain
Of the plain. And my troops, they would try
To become jungle cocks and to train
In the lore of the bush and to vie
With the Nagas in ways to regain
All the land they had lost and belie
The belief that the Japs would remain

Ever more. But my men had to ply
Through the jungle and swamps, in the rain,
In the mud, up the mountains, and lie
With the leeches and would seldom complain;
But their weapons and packs made them sigh
For the fleet naked Naga's disdain
Of the luggage of war and lines of supply,
Or for boots on their feet or for strain
On their backs. For as light as a fly
With no weight to impinge or enchain
Or impede, like the birds of the sky
They were free, and as free would remain
In their Manipur hills when the stain
Of this yellow dye fades from the eye,
At the end of this Burmese campaign.

Song

Written after a frustrating visit - 8 hours on train each way - to Katy

Down south we went to swim and laze,
With sun tan cream and bathing gear;
But all we saw for fourteen days
Was wind and rain. Thank God for beer!
Next time I think we'll take our rest
At Burton-on-the-Trent. It's near,
The air is Beery, Beer the Best,
So drink and sing for all to hear
Thank God for Beer!

1950

KATE'S BIRTHDAY

It would be most immoderate
To calculate your age, dear Kate;
And quite unfair to name the date
That comes too late for forty-eight
Or even forty-nine. Yet fate,
Divine, has intervened to state
Your passing through the half-way gate
To Heaven's Shrine. So let this great
Occasion now commemorate
And celebrate this day. The plate
Is full of birthday cake; the crate
Of wine and beer is there to circulate
As all our friends, intoxicate
The air with their affectionate
Regards. We kiss you Kate!

GOOD ADVICE
AND SOLEMN WARNING
TO AN INEXPERIENCED GIRL

Now pretty girls of slender girth
Who seem to men most whistle-worth
Must be informed that males are fickle
And know the code of kisseltickle.
For spooning when the moon is brightest
Can tend to make the heart excitus;
So keep his hand above the belt
Though they be soft as meltyfelt.
Keep knees together, blow your nose
Bore him with some Browning prose
And soon he'll wane and learn to be
Respectful to a Teenoldshe.
When springtime floats across the park
He'll hark the lark and start to spark
And take you to a leafy dell
And tell you that you're loveabelle;
But keep your head and say the grass
Is far too damp for comfortlass.
If on a bench he begs you to sit
And starts to paw and panderbit
Just take your compact out and paste
Your face with cool concern to chaste

His lust away. Perhaps long up
A lonely lane his car will splut
And groan. Tell him to take his tool
Kit out or find a poolafuel.
For you know well of his foul scheme
To keep you for a night of seam!
And if, upon a summers day,
He walks you through the nonnyhay
And pauses when he has a stitch,
Begins to puff and panty-itch,
Beside a stack - another plot!
Just say he has a paunchypot!
And stride away. He may entice
You out to see a film of vice,
Debauchery and porn. Beware,
My dear, of such invites to snare
You in his kinky lair to view
Some sordid scenes of sex, too blue
And bad for eyes of innocence.
If you do go and take offence
At what you see, then rise and say
There is no way you wish to stay
And witness such appalling lust !
And tell him that his breath is just
As nasty as his mind, a smell
Dispelling death to any well
Behaved young gell's romantic love.
Then leave; but also leave your glove;
He will return it soon to prove
He still has hopes and will improve

And make you groovy glad. He's sure
To lure you to his flat to jawre
About his videos; but when
He pours out alcohol you pren
You've taken up the pledge that day.
And settle for a cupotay
(But watch he does not slip in phiz
A pill to make you sillywiz)!
What ever happens do not let
Him catch you with his etchy - net.
These etchings hang above his bed
But once in there I've had my sed
Because, worst luck, I've never been
So close to such a sordid scene.

MEG

My blood runs deep from Indus springs
My hair flows from the Nile,
My raven eyes and silver rings
Enhance a Magyar smile.
I lived the close zingaro life
On heath, and moor and fell
Till I became a tinker's wife -
A story sad to tell.
At seventeen on Epsom night
We danced the dark away,
The fiddles set the moon alight
To welcome Derby day.
I stamped my feet in Spanish style,
I moved with Moorish grace
And flashed my lips into a smile,
When I first saw his face!
His eyes were crying out for mine
Ablaze with heart's desire,
He joined with me like Columbine
To dance around the fire.
We crept inside his caravan
Well stocked with stolen stores,
Where he explained his pleasing plan
For killing household chores.
He made me cook him ham and egg
And scrape his stubbly chin,
I called him Claude, he called me Meg,
And softly sank the gin.
At night in bed he laid his head
Upon my cherried chest
And when the amber turned to red
I knew I'd passed my test.

And so it was that I became
A scrap-iron dealer's doll,
And lived a life of leisured shame
Well oiled with alcohol.
In catacombs he ransacked tombs
For gold and brass and lead
And filched, while fresh, the flowering blooms
From graves of newly dead.
He fed the fish in fountain lakes
With gum that glued up gills
And drugged St. James ducks and drakes
With tranquillizer pills.
He found the church of old St Paul's
A pigeon's perching home
And poisoned them with pastry balls
Arranged around the dome,
He poached for peacocks in the park
For feathers flogged for fans,
And pinched from pockets in the dark
Top secret service plans –
And these he'd trade for Chinese jade
Or sold for Russian gold,
For Claude the Card, and Claude the Blade,
Was bad as he was bold.
He was indeed the Devil's mate
A skunk in a monk's attire
Who pinched the parson's pewter plate
While singing in the choir.
To drink pink gin and sin in mink
And slink with tingling trinks
Is fine until one starts to think
Of magistrates and clinks.
So while I sang a gypsy chant
I grabbed his precious stones

And pushed dear Claude inside the plant
For pulverizing bones.
Then in a funk away I slunk
And staggered up the road
With Claude the junk-man in the trunk
To hush the jingling load.
I strode, I rode, by tram and train
And tube and taxi ride
To London airport for a plane
To land beyond the Clyde.
And there I keep a decent house
For tourists to the moors
Who wish to try their guns at grouse
Or reeling on the floors.
And now dear Claude the card at last
Does justice to his birth
And pays for his appalling past
By fertilizing earth.

THE FUR TRAPPER'S WIFE

Song: Canadian Scene

A wave of the hand,
A sob in the throat,
Farewell, lovely land;
God speed, little boat!

She turns with a sigh
And sinks down to pray,
For signs in the sky
Show storms in the bay.

That night by the shore
The bitter winds blow,
And trees by the score
Fall dead in the snow.

The storm dies at dawn,
The woods settle down,
Now smooth as a lawn
The bay's lost its frown.

The tide in its turn
Caresses the sand;
The sun comes to burn
New life in the land.

The first sign of spring,
The squirrels swing high
And birds start to sing
To winters last sigh.

The skies that were grey
Are blue and serene;
The snow dies way
And white becomes green.

A haven of peace
Except in her heart
For storms do not cease
When loved ones depart.

CHANGE OF AIR - 1964

It appears that there's been,
If one goes by reports,
Quite a change in the scene
At our sea-side resorts.
For the 'U's' used to stay
At the 'Splendide' and 'Crown'
Overlooking the bay
And away from the town;
While the middle-class - stayed
At the 'Grove' and the 'Grand
A bit off the parade
Yet so near to the sand.
But for those who had slaved,
In that class ridden age,
And with sacrifice saved
From a meek weekly wage,
There were rooms and high tea
With a view of the pier
And a sniff of the sea,
And aromas of beer.
Now the tables are turned
And receptionists bow
To the workers they spurned
Who are their betters now.
Oh! the buffets and bars
Are decanting rare wines
And are selling cigars,
To the men from the mines,
While their dainty wives slink
Round the lounges and halls
Overflowing with mink

And begemmed for the balls.
Now Milady and Lord
Are so taxed and so poor
They just cannot afford
The sea-side anymore.
So they sell tea and cakes
Off their best silver plate
Or do guide work and take
Silver tips by the gate
Of their castles. They pray
For their takings to bring
Enough florins to pay
For a fling in the Spring
In Paree. But the cream
Of this land (who are those
In between the extreme
('U' and 'Low') now repose
In the prim stinging hive
Of the boarding house bee,
Who continues to thrive
Without workers or drones
Who've deserted her rooms
For the tonier zones
Of the town. And she zooms
All around with the airs
Of a dame, for her dream
Has come true and her prayers
Have been met - she's now queen
Of the white collar type.
These are never profane
At the clangorous pipe,
Or the pong of the drain
Or complain if the chains
Do not pull. So, it's plain

That the boffin and brains
Are the landlady's gain,
And the beer bottle stains
And the stubs on the floors
Are exchanged for *The Times*
And the third programme bores
With their lagers and limes.
At the 'Splendide' you now
Can have kippers at four;
At the 'Crown' they allow
One to 'rock' on the floor,
And a new atmosphere
With a saltier sting
Has enlivened, I hear,
The resorts. So now sing
All ye workers a most
Merry song, giving praise
For the change on our coast!

'My Man Fred'

A Welsh cob gelding, fifteen hands,
On powerful hocks, well down,
His body deep and strong he stands,
His coat a velvet brown.

His crest is arched and broad his chest
And pretty is his head,
Of all my hunters he's the best,
His name is 'My Man Fred.'

For fourteen seasons with Quorn
He heard the dog-hounds speak,
And heard the huntsman wind his horn
Two hunting days a week.

On Charnwood's trappy Tuesday side
His leaps were nimble, deft, feline,
He took the stone walls in his stride,
And most. mistakes were mine.

We had our falls, or I was thrown,
And sometimes things went wrong
When forcing Fred when he was blown,
Or we stayed out too long.

There is no cure at twenty four
For tendons strained or weak,
I dare not hunt Fred any more
As bones begin to creak

But Fred is very busy still
And helps the school with pride,
And shows great sympathy and skill
In teaching kids to ride.

He squeals and snorts when he's let out
And rolls in mud or dust,
But when the hounds are round about
No fence is safe to trust!

A Blank Verse to a Blank Man, D.H.L. who says:

I thank whatever gods' there be to guide
Me through life's maze, for granting me a sure
And concrete soul; for never have I felt
The need to plead relief from pain, or cry
Self-pity's tears. I've faced my fortunes, good
And bad with carefree fortitude and sealed
Up scars with scorn. I hear there lies ahead
A haunt where conscience must be cleansed; but Hell
Can burn to cinders, and the Heavens turn
To ash for all I care. No bait can tempt
Me from my course, I'll never kneel to fear;
Let others quake; my fate's at my command,
I'll take what comes without a whine and keep
My soul intact and take whatever comes.

LOVE IN AN AIR RAID

Grand Central Hotel Room, bombed and wrecked.

Oh Twinkle Toes! Oh Love's Delight!
I long to lie with you tonight.
With you so near I will not care
When air raids pound; nor will I hear
The all-clear sound, for in your arms
I will be deaf to all alarms.
Nothing will dampen down the fire
Of love we feel or curb desire.
We will not fear for anything
But share what ever fate may bring.

1941

(Came down, fire escape in morning - never heard a thing !)

Miss Fell

A party given by Joyce Glover and Grace Dalton
for Miss Fell of Yeldersley Hall, Derbyshire.

Your party, Joyce, did quite excel

All other balls

In country halls.

Your party, Grace, went very well

The food was grand

And *what* a band!

The wine was sweet as Muscatel,

Thank you so much

For such and such!

But now I must confess to tell

To my disgrace

I could not place

The gracious face of Mistress Fell,

So thanks from me

When next you see

The birthday Gell of Yeldersley.

1960's

K. K. J.

More at home at a suite in the Hilton,
With panache and great dash she ran Milton
And lived in some style
In that elegant pyle
On Champagne and oysters and Stilton.

Good legs for a boot, a beautiful face,
This agent is Queen of the chase,
Her elegant style
Is known every mile
For her hands and her seat and her Grace.

Without any rudeness or guile,
All around this elegant pile,
She puts tenants at ease
In her efforts to please
With her wonderful welcoming smile.

STARDUST

For John (6½)

My Daddy's flying very soon
Up high to outer space
And hopes to land upon the moon
To build a polar base.

The moon's a million miles away.
I wonder what he'll find ?
They say the moon men have a ray
That make our earth men blind.

But Daddy has a secret store
Of magic wonder pills
Which bring back sight to eyes once more
And cures all cosmic ills.

From base he'll fly to other stars
And sail celestial seas
And maybe meet the men from Mars
 And see old Hercules.

From days of old the eye of man
Have scanned the solar skies
And tried to find how earth began
And where their heaven lies.

My Daddy will at last unfold
The secrets of the spheres
And, maybe, when the tale is told,
The shape of future years

Nonsense Verses

At Torquay and Frinton-on-Sea
One cannot have kippers for tea,
And beer at the bar
Is too common by far
So its Southend or Clacton for me !

* * *

The wife of a sailor at Looe
Was a nagging old hag of a shrew,
So they used her for bait
To land the best weight
Of sharks, ever caught by the crew.

* * *

A lonely soul
Should take a stroll
To the cliff's of Dover
And jump over.

* * *

The Churches would rather fight
 Than unite,
Far better they pray
To act God's way.

* * *

Dr Nkruma
Would sooner
Have Ghana
Like Havana,
Red and Black,
Than Ike and Mac.

*   *   *

What hope
For those who smoke?
The answer,
Cancer.

*   *   *

Mama thought young Jim unclean
And put him In the wash machine
When she held him to the light
She found him far more blue than white.

*   *   *

CELTIC IDYLL,
BREEDON-ON-THE-HILL

On Breedon's windswept hill the sheep
Alone have grazed its waves of green
That curl around the slopes too steep
For plough and drill. But here, between
The Church's wall and Bulwarks mound,
A field of golden oats caress
The only plot of level ground.
And here, when young, I brought old Bess,
My Suffolk Punch, to plough and till
The sacred soil, so sweet to smell
When freshly turned. I heard the shrill
And shriek of falling gulls that fell
Upon the loam. The skylarks sang
Cascades of song, rising high
And sinking low. The church bell rang
A muffled toll to sanctify
A gathered soul. And as I walked
Behind my mare I came aware
That shadows of the past now stalked
The land as though the brittle share
Had spoiled their sleep or angered bold,
Germanic Gods, or raised, from deep
Encrustments, spirits from the old
Idolatry; and from their sleep
On butterbur and shepherds purse
The goblins, elves, and fairy folk
In panic fled with spells to curse
The plough. Warlock's and witches woke
To perch upon the cradle tower

Of Breedon Church and croak as crows.
Black Anna left her bony bower
And Hobbes left his hole (He knows,
They say, a magic way that makes
The Butter change from milk, and calls
At night, to help on farms and bakes
The bread at dawn; but trouble falls
On any dairy-maid who fails
To leave an apron clean for him
To wear; then milk is sour'd and pails
Are filled with tears. But Anna, grim
And ghoulish hag, was bad
As any vampire bat and said
To wear a cloak of silk and had
A pointed hat upon her head
And pointed teeth, and fed, at night
On baby's blood if she could find
It's bed. So when time came to light
The lamps and draw the parlour blind,
All windows were then shut up tight
Until the welcome morn returned).
The folding furrows speckled bright
With artifacts the plough had churned
Up from below, the ancient ware
Of early man, the winking glint
Of beads of glass, the duller glare
Of blades of bronze, a flashing flint,
An arrow head, a whet-stone cleaved
From Carvers rock, a broken urn,
A comb of bone that may have weaved
A Saxon loom, a grit-stone guern
That once had ground some Celtic Corn;
A Roman coin, a copper nail,
A bridle cheekpiece made of horn,

A green stone axe from Great Langdale
In Cumberland and many sherds
Of Suffolk clay; and yellow bones
Of Celtic Cows on whose red herds
The Roman legions fed; and stones
Lay scattered round the ground the sad
Remains of shattered sacrilege;
For once, as Breedon's cross, they had
In glory stood between the ridge
And wall, and fell to Pagan Dane.
The cross, in Celtic style, was tall
And carved by Mercian Monks with chain
And spiral coil motifs and small
Reliefs of Saints, and built before
The Celtic Church to Roman thrall
Declined. The weather changed, a roar
Of thunder frightened Bess, a squall
Of biting wind and rain compelled
Retreat. I quickly ran to crawl
Behind a stack of hay and held
The reins, a sack about my back.
The lightening flashed across the sea
Of seething, swirling waves of black
Tormented clouds. A single tree,
An ancient yew, that grew among
The graves was well within my view.
I watched as twisting branches swung
To-and-fro and rose and fell askew
And bent before the bitter storm;
Then suddenly began to see
That something strange in human form
Was taking shape beneath the tree.
I strained my eyes and in the glare
Of lightening thought I saw a man

Materialise, with reddish hair
And blazing eyes. I quickly ran
Towards the wall to get as near
As I dare to be. And there I peered
In fear, and saw a man as clear
As eyes can see, and he appeared
To stare at me with eyes of hate.
A sword was hanging from his side
His right hand held a spear, a great
Big shield was on his back, of hide
And willow made. His crimson cloak
Perhaps had come from some dead son
Of Rome. He did not move and spoke
No word; his eyes alone the one
And only spark of life that made
This man appear alive. And those
Two eyes, when all began to fade,
Remained alight and did not close;
But suddenly began to glide
Towards my hide with shrieking cries;
I watched the wings outstretched and wide,
And saw the beak; yet still those eyes
Belonged to human form a-glow
With angry fires. They were the same
I saw upon the face below
The tree, and as this spectre came,
I felt the autumn air grow cold
And shivered at the sudden change.
I dived below the wall and rolled
Beneath a bush and heard the strange
Unearthly bird with talons scrape
The coping stone above my head,
And thanked the lord for my escape
From steel-like claws, and prayed the dread

Revolting evil owl had flown
Away for good. The icy air
Gave way to warmth. The storm had blown
The clouds and rain away; my mare
And plough at work again; I thought
Of all the things I'd seen that hour,
That man, that bird that nearly caught
My eyes, the supernatural power
Which changed and charged the atmosphere.
He was no Roman, Saxon, Dane
No Norman, Roundhead, Cavalier,
That stood beneath that tree, so vain
So proud, so full of hate. I felt
A presence I would see again,
The spirit of a sullen Celt;
A chief, perhaps, who died in pain
Or gave his life to hold
This Coritani Holy Hill
From Belgae Bands or Romans bold
Or internecine feuds, and will
Not sleep if stranger's tools disturb
His hallowed soil. He wakes to fight
Again with Druid spells to curb
Intruders on his ground. That night
I walked again upon the crest
Of Breedon Hill, and walked with care,
And quietly, as though a guest
On some monastic lawn; and there
Was not a soul to see. I heard
A faint yet haunting sound come out
The old yew tree as if a bird
Had learnt to play the harp. I doubt
I'll hear again such sounds as those
That rose like soft Aeolian strings

Or when the water-music flows
In moorland rills or mountain springs;
Or like the Pibrock's sad lament
In highland glens or Irish vales
That tell of lonely exile spent
Abroad, of tragedy and tales
About the death of kings and chiefs.
That harp, perhaps, performed its art
To help St. Hardulp's stern beliefs,
And, may-be, St. Modwenna's heart
Was torn on hearing its refrains,
Reminding her of Iral's land
In Iveagh's Hills and distant strains
Of Irish pipes, and Patrick's hand
Upon her head, and harps of Gaels
On Callan's banks that told the tales
Of Tara's Hall. No nightingales
At harvest time singing wassails
To greet the garnered corn could sing
So sweet as music made that night.
I thought of Aethelred, the king,
Who built the church and then, despite
His wealth and power and vast estate,
Became a monk. Who knows? he may
Have walked just here to meditate
And heard the heavenly sounds one day
And knew their meaning well. I thought
Of Breedon Princeps Frithuric
The founding Father-Prior who brought
To Breedon wealth and fantastic
Endowments of hides. Did he,
At eventide, this music hear?
Did Tatwin stand beneath the tree
When just a Breedon Monk, and peer

Into its dark green folds to see
The fountain of the muse? and when
He took that greatest See
Of Canterbury did he not then
In riddles pen about the pure
Enchanting tunes of paradise?
Perhaps its true, the siren lure
Of harpist strings only entice
A Celtic soul, and Pibrock's dirge
Will only merge with Celtic Blood.
I'm sure that by some darkling purge
On Cornwall's craggy coast where stood
Sir Tristrem with his fair Ysonde
This music made their loving good,
And, at their deaths in deep despond,
They heard this last cadenza flood
Away their floating souls beyond
The Vale of Avalon.

1930

Notes

1.   ST. MODWENNA was an Irish Saint, daughter of Maucteus,
King of Iveagh. After being blessed by St. Patrick and after many missionary
adventures in Ireland, she came to England during the early 6th Century She
is said to have met the Breedon Anchorite and patron saint St. Hardulph and
founded a religious house at Burton-on-Trent, where the parish church is
dedicated to her and St. Mary. She died in Scotland where she had founded
other houses in 518 and was buried at Burton-on-Trent.

2.   St. Hardulph. He is said to be an Anglican or Mercian Prince Who

became an anchorite and religious teacher living in Anchor Caves close to the Trent near Foremarke. He is patron saint of Breedon on-the-Hill.Leicestershire.

3.   Tatwin. A Breedon-on-the-Hill monk who became Archbishop of Canterbury in 731. He was fond of writing enigmas in latin hexameters and was considered one of the best Anglo-Norman poets, as well as a learned priest. He died in 734. Breedon, when he was there, had a great scriptoria and library of priceless books and manuscripts. In 874 it was sacked by the Danes wintering at Repton.

4.   Hobbes. To the North East of the Hill is a field called Hobbes Hole, from which a hidden cave is said to run under the hill in which a mysterious little man was said to live. He would come out at night and help churn the milk and do other chores so long as a clean apron awaited him. I remember a small cave N.E. of the church on the face of the old disused quarry on the left of the Wilson Road, which was known as Hobbes Hole.

5.   Black Anna. Sometimes called Black Annis or Agnes, or Cat Anna or Cat Annis. In Leicester itself the legend of Black Anna goes back into the mists of Celtic lore, she was particularly associated with the Dane Hills area where there was a cave known as Black Annas Bower or Bower Close. She was said to live in Pollarded oaks or clefts in rocks and caves. She was said to attack children and scratch them to death with her claws, suck their blood and hang their skins out to dry. On Easter Monday it used to be a tradition for the Mayor and his officers to meet at Black Anna's Bower Close and hunt a drag of cat skin (cat Annis) representing a hare, with hounds, back to the mayor's parlour. This custom died out about 1767; but the festival occasion lingered on for years with the fair on Easter Monday at Dane Hills.

She was also supposed to inhabit a cellar beneath Leicester Castle from which she returned to Dane Hills by a secret tunnel). In Nichol's history of Leicestershire, he quotes Burton about the legend of a 15th century tablet in Swithland Church to one Agnes Scott. Shaw was apparently an Anchoress who lived in a cave (Antrurn). He includes a poem about Black Annis, written by Lieutenant John Heyrick:

Tis said the foul of mortal man recoil's
To view Black Annis eye, so fierce and wild;
Vast talons, foul with human flesh, there grew
In place of hands, and features livid blue,
Glared in her visage; whilst her obscene waist
Warns skins of human victims close embraced.

(This sounds very like the creature that cae at me from out of the yew tree)

The Anna legend probably goes back to Celtic times. In Celtic Ireland Dana or Ana (Don in Welsh) is mother Goddess of the race of Tuatha De Danann. Ireland was known as 'the land of Anann' and near Killarney - there are the paps of Anann', Bretons call them dead 'Anaon' (the departed) and several places were named after Anna who, like the Leicestershire one, was said to be a man-eater and guardian of the dead. The cult of the Black Virgin and Saint Anne gradually became channeled in to the Christian worship of the virgin's mother.

J Markale in his *Celtic Civilisation* devotes several pages to the mother Goddess who is also referred to in Anna Ross's *Pagan Celtic Britain*.

6.   Carver's Rock. Near Melbourne, Leicestershire. The Romans used this stone for sharpening swords, scythe, etc.

7.   A gurge is a swirling pool.

DONINGTON OAK

The changing scene beneath the shadow of an oak tree in Donington
Park, Leicestershire and Breedon-on-the-Hill, Leicestershire.

Where Trent his mazy currents pours
And Donington's old oaks to every breeze
Whisper the tale of by-gone centuries.
Thomas Moore.

I'm hollow now inside, and pains,
That come with age, cause limbs to groan
A little more. The snow, the rains
And heat, oft make me loud bemoan
My fallen boughs. Yet still my bark
Is thick, my heart is sound and strong
My seed. The pride of all the park
I've been for centuries so long
That even man acclaims me Queen,
And spares the axe and saw. What tales
1 could recount! What sights I've seen
Around my throne! s Time slid but snails
Pace past my bole and hardly changed
The Domesday scene. The Deer still stride
In vales of green which once were ranged
By Robin Hood, and Knights would ride
Beneath these Oaks with Hawk and Hound,
And bow and spear. Inside me, red
With rust old arrow heads are found
That failed to find their fleshy bed.
With Later days there came new ways
Of shooting dead shy game. With shot
And flame flew balls of lead to blaze

And maim. Now sprays of angry hot
Red pellets spit at birds on wing
Pour down a rain of sudden pain
And bring a stinging patterned ring
Of scars to perforate my grain.
Each day, it seems, man's fertile mind
Produces something strange and new;
Yet still, I find, there stays behind
A strain of atavistic hue,
That feeds the need of man to meet
And challenge raw unfettered seas
And mountains, jungles, swamps, to beat
What ever dangers that he sees.
In times of peace a Knight had still
Trained for war and keep his horse
And body fit, retain this skill
Of horsemanship and keep in force
His men of arms. The very same
Related skills applied to arts
The huntsman needs to catch his game,
In hawking partridges in parks,
In casting hounds to scent their prey;
Or stalking in the hills for buck,
And aiming at the stag at bay,
Or catching fish and geese and duck.
In ancient times the noble Celts
Came hunting round these sacred oaks
For winter food and skins, and pelts
For blankets, carpets, tents and cloaks.
The beaver, badger, boar and bear,
The wolf and wildcat, weasel, fox,
The marten, stoat and proud red deer,
The shy roe buck and auroch ox
And fierce wild swine - All these and more,

Were here before a Caesar came
To goad the men in woad to war;
And build their roads and tame
The tribes. They held so dear
The British bear they bore them live
To Rome for gladiator duels:
They made the fertile farmland thrive,
And brought in better farming tools;
And rich was trade with overseas,
With Gaul in grain and skins and wood.
When Rome itself was on it's knees
With vandals at her door, the blood
Tie called the legions back to home.
The vacuum caused by their withdrawal
Upset the ordered ways of Rome,
And British chiefs began to brawl
In internecine feuds or lapse
In easy lassitude. Too late
They heard the Saxon horn, and taps
Of Jutish drum! As if by fate,
The straight and solid Roman ways
Made easy all advance. From east
The Angles slowly made inlays
To marshy fens and men and beast
Were brought ashore by Frisian boat
Or put on wooden rafts to gain
Access to inland plains and float
To fight the sullen Celts. In vain
The British tribes attacked the strong
Germanic bands whose forbears came
In Roman times to raid along
The Saxon shore. Some stayed to claim
The land to farm, or trade, and swore
To keep the peace. Yet more were paid

By chiefs for aid in helping shore
Up their defence from Pictish raid
Or Scots attack or tribal fight.
But some rebelled and formed a horde
Against the British clans and set alight
The countryside and put to sword
Or took as slaves all those who dared
To cross their path. Around these parts
The Coritani Celts prepared
Defensive forts on high ramparts
At Burrough camp and Beacon mound,
And Bardon crown and Breedon Hill,
And Billesdon and earth works round
Old Roman posts. But naught could still
The stream of Angles up the Wreake
And Welland, Soar and Trent, on wave
On wave they came. To soft and weak
With Roman peace, however brave,
Those Celtic tribes went to the hills
To save their heritage with blame
To Roman roads for all the ills
Befallen them, and sulk in shame;
And plague had struck the countryside
As well as Teutons, Scots and Picts.
They lacked the leadership to guide
A common cause to cease conflict
Among themselves. From Culdee times
They knew of Christ, and high in fells
And western hills and Cornish climes
Where Druid rods still ruled, the cells
Of Celtic monks, and anchorites
And learned men, slowly replaced
Of ancient shrines and mithraic sites;
And soon most Celtic tribes embraced

This Church. When darkness stalked the land
And Europe lay in strife - The light
Still shone in cells of stone; the hand
Of God was there, alone to fight
The Pagan hold. Monastic hives
Of worker monks with parchment, paints
And quill and brush, rewrote the lives
Of holy men, disciples, saints
And kings, were dimmed and darkness came and Prince
Arthur, Vortigern, Ambrosius
Became but goodnight tales. Since
Then, Christians of Pelagius
Proclaimed their message through the land.
And Austin and Paulinus brought,
In later times, another brand
Of worship and at Southwell taught
To end all pagan ways. At last
The wild Teutonic tribes were tame
And Hengest and Horsa's fame now past
To bed-time tales like Arthur's name,
Or sang at court in sad refrain
By strolling minstrels telling tales
Of daring deeds and great campaigns,
Of gallant Knights and Holy Grails.
The Anglo Saxon Mercian Kings
Encouraged art and learning, verse,
And Christian ways and all the things
That peace can bring when clear the curse
Of war. But once again the wheel
Of history turned and just as they,
Decades ago, had come to steal
And burn the British homes and slay
The placid tribes; so now they felt
The Viking steel upon the throat

Of peace as prowling sea-wolves dealt
To them as they had Britons smote.
For years the Danish pirates poured
From waterways to pillage church
And shrine and Manor House. They moor'd
At Repton many months to rest and search
The land for loot and food; and sacked
This seat of Mercian kings and burned
The palace down and even hacked
To ground the Abbey Cross and turned
The town to ruins. They packed the plate
Of church and state in boats along the Trent
To send back home as worthy spoils to wait
For their return. And with them went
The fairest slaves and silk and books
They could not read, and bangles, beads
And silver rings and crosses, crooks
And coins, and gold and parchment deeds.
The Breedon monks in terror fled
Their monastery, founded by the King
And Saint, Aethelred, that bred
The great Tatwine who wore the ring
And cross of Canterbury. They left
The monastery a shell and broke
The panels, carvings, cross, cleft
By monks of Saxon stock yet spoke
With Celtic undertones and showed
That Mercian craft in stones portrayed
A cultured race whose sculptures glowed
In bold creative art that paid
Regards to ancient roots that gave
The race its tree. The vines and grapes,
The Pelta Shields, the chains and the wave
Of Grecian keys; fantastic shapes

Of Saxon scrolls, the birds that feast
On grapes, the lion, and jars of wine,
The strutting cocks, the Anglian beast,
The panel frieze of scrolls of vine
That intertwine like columbine
In Celtic spiral coral design;
The Breedon Angel in her shrine
Her right hand raised to bless her flock
In true Byzantine grace, that came
With Theodore of Tarsus's crook
To Canterbury, when Breedon's fame
Was very young, a hundred years
Before the Danes. The beasts on shelves
Kept guard all night, allayed the fears
The Saxons felt for evil elves
And demon snakes - and dragons stayed
Awake till dawn to fight and stay
The devils of the dark. The griffins preyed
On goblin creatures of the day,
And, on the ledge, the centaurs played
And pranced like lambs; but kept at bay
The hungry hounds of hell who laid
In wait to kill who came to pray;
Yet loved to lick the witch warlock
And Black Annis who'd often take
Them bones. The 'Virgin of the Rock'
Was carved perhaps to keep awake
Modwenna's memory. She came
Across the Irish sea to search
For Breedon's patron saint whose fame
Had filtered far from Breedon's church
In anchor cave which he had scraped
From rock just like a catacomb
Of Rome; or like the cells they shaped

From sandy stone to meeting room
In Asia Minor after the call
Disciples made on Greeks to tell
Of Christ. St. Hardulph, like St. Paul,
Discarded his material shell
For one of spiritual desire.
In Saint Modwenna, blessed nun,
There burnt the same unselfish fire
To serve the poor, and with this son
Of Bernicia's King she warmly shared
So much in prayer and life; for both
Were noble, meek, and neither cared
For comforts and had pledged the oath
Of poverty, both wore the ring
Of chastity, both were scholars,
Both of Royal birth (she the king
Of Iveagh's child) both had scars
Of suffering and pain and each
Had faithful followers who walked
The countryside to preach and teach;
Both had healing powers and talked
To God as though a friend. When young,
This modest girl of grace displayed
Unusual healing gifts among
Her race of Irial Gaels. She made
Her way to Ardmacha and paid
St. Patrick homage and he laid
His hands upon her head and prayed
With her and baptised this frail maid
Of Iveagh in a pond which gave,
They say, it healing power. She stayed
To listen and to learn the brave
And saintly way he lived, betrayed
Enslaved, a sailor, student, priest

Who had survived such fearful odds.
St. Modwenn then returned back east
And knew the path to tread to God's
Own house. At Faugher she began
To build a church, and at her side
Were seven maids from out her clan
And one who was a Royal bride,
A widow with an infant son
Who later on became a King.
They often saw their work undone,
Their houses burnt and everything
They had, destroyed. They sometimes starved
And once survived for many days
On bark from trees. And what was carved
In Breedon church, I think, portrays
This nun and by her side her eight
Disciple sister saints. And, seen
Outside the church, a cross, with great
Merovingian beasts; a screen
Depicting Bible scenes, a Celt
On horse, with spear - all this fine art
Was smashed apart when Hubba dealt
His hammer blows at Breedon's heart
And Henguar set up Odin, Frey
And Thor and had all priests expelled
Or killed. The conquering Danes made way
Along the Trent and Wreake and held
The towns, as plague and hunger stalked
The land. The King, Burgred, and fled
Abroad and men looked back, and talked
Of better days and better gods, and shed
Their Christian ways; and many turned
To ancient German Gods (akin
To those of Danes), whom they had spurned

In Paeda's time when monks carne in
To Repton town. Now men did sing
Of Erce, Eostre, Nethus and Thor
And Itretha, Woden, Tew and Ing.
The Saxon puppet, Ceolwulf, wore
The crown, though Halfden was the king,
And Danelaw ruled for forty years.
As good King Alfred fought to fling
Guthrum from Wessex, people's fears
Of never seeing English power
Return again were far less rife,
And Lady Ethelflaed, the flower
Of England, inspiring wife
Of Ethelred, the Earldorman
Of Mercia, re-kindled the spark
Of ancient pride. Then Athelstan
Her brother's son, who had the mark
Of Mercia imprinted long
Upon his youth, united both
The Kingdoms. Later came the strong
And wise King Edgar and the growth
Of monasteries throughout the land;
Next Ethelred's unhappy reign,
Upset by Svein's determined band
Of Danes, and by the mark of Cain,
Left England tired of civil strife;
And poor from Danegeld blackmail bribes,
And sacrifice of too much life
In battles with those Nordic tribes.
And on St. Brice's day there came
Another shadow on his name,
When Ethelred, to his great shame,
Decided every Dane fair game
For Saxon sword; and peaceful Dane,

And Christian Dane and were killed throughout
The south and Svein's own sister slain.
Old Forkbeard and Thorkell went out
For due revenge and ravaged wide
The countryside and Ethelred
Retired to France until Svein died;
And then returned, but soon was dead;
And war was carried on between
The son of Svein, Canute, and son
Of Ethelred, Edmund. The green
And fertile fields of Ashington
Were turned to bloody red when these
Two fought their final fight
That bought the English to their knees
And killed the flower of English might.
It seemed as though a curse was laid
Upon the English as Wulfstan
Had warned would happen when he made
Impassioned pulpit pleas to fan
The dying flames of loyalty, trust
In Christian faith, in pride, courage,
Condeming all the greed and lust
And deeds of shame and false marriage.
Soon after Ashington, Ironside
Had died and King Canute became
The only king. The wretched tide
Of war and famine ceased, and tame
Became the warrior Dane as all
Become as Christian as their King,
And Wulfstan and Thorkell the tall
Would help Canute with care to bring
The country to just laws. For he
Was King of Denmark too,
And Norway, and controlled the sea

And half of Sweden's land, and who
Was recognised as overlord
By Scotland and by Wales. The Queen
Was, too, a key to good accord
And harmony as she had been
The Queen Of Ethelred and bore
Him Prince Alfred and Prince Edward,
And to her second King she gave
A Prince, HarthCanute; she tried hard
To have this son made heir to save
The twenty years of peace and law
The Danish interlude had brought
To English shores, that changed the raw
And pagan Dane into a sort
Of Christian Englishman, her name
Was Aelfgifu-Emma, 'The Gem
Of the Normans' who became
"The Lady of Winchester". This stem
Of ancient Norman stock and life
Of England's roots had to accept
Another Aelfgifu, the wife
Or 'More Danico' he kept
In Scandinavia and known
As 'Aelfgifu of Northampton'.
Across the Northern Sea was blown
A scandalous saga to poison
The inheritance of her sons.
The rumours claimed she never bore
A child and went for heirs to nuns
Who kept unwanted babes. She swore
These stories false and that her Svein
And Harold came from Canute's seed
And from her womb. And when the rein
Of King Cnut was over, greed

For power among the claimants made
England unhappy once again
As fraternal squabbles preyed
Upon the peaceful land. The main
Support for Harthcnut was from
Emma and Earl Godwin. He spent
Too long trying to overcome
His rival in Norway; This meant
That Aelfgifu could press the claim
Far Harold Harefoot (her son Svein
Had died). Leofric thought the same
And so did all the northern Theyns;
So Harold Harefoot duly came;
But not before he stained his reign's
Record with Royal blood to shame
The name of Danes for years. With pain
And torture he had killed the poor
Defenceless Prince Alfred, the son
Of Emma who had come ashore
From France to stay with her. The one
He trusted most, the Earl Godwin
Betrayed his charge to Harold's men.
The king's uncertain reign within
Four years was over. It was then
The long delayed ascension came
Of Harth Canute whose only claim
To goodness was to link his name
With Edward and to share the same
Uneasy throne. He, too, died young
And with him died the last of King
Canute's old line. But he who'd sprung
From Alfred's stock was there to bring
An English crown to rule again.
Edward had lived in France too long

But Godwin kept the power behind
The throne and reinforced his strong
Control by marriage made to bind
His family to Edward's house,
His daughter, fair Edith, became
The Queen and his son, Harold's spouse,s
Was sister to the King. The fame
Of Godwin grew. He also had
Six other sons, half Danish and
All strong and powerful men, tall bad
And cruel, but brave as lions. This band
Of Godwin's caused the pious King
Unhappiness of mind and made
Him wary, too, remembering
His brother's fate under the shade
Of Godwin's care. His reign was hurt
By wrong advice within his court
And Norman intrigue and inert
Action on his own part that brought
Back raids from Irish Danes, and Wales
And pirates from the sea, and worst
Of all, from Godwin. With the scales,
So weighed against them they dispersed
Abroad to gather strength and then
Returned with vengeance and before
Too long had back his power, his men
Replacing Norman courtiers for
They were banished from the realm.
When Godwin died Harold was all
But under-king and took the helm
To ward off foes and helped install
A standing army to repel
Invasion. Strong he was and loyal,
A faithful soldier loved as well

By Danes and English, who, with royal
Approval, relieved his saintly king
Of martial duties, but kept him
As busy as could be, hawking
Hunting game. But times were grim
When news was spread about the sad
Demise of Edward. The Aetheling
Was next in line; but still a lad.
The Witan felt the need to bring
The best and bravest man to head
The country through this troubled time
Of change and intrigue; one whose steed
And shield could stem the threats of prime
Contenders, from Denmark, Norway
And Normandy. The Witan chose
Harold Godwin, and straight away
He raised his house of Carls and those
Freemen from Wapentakes, the Fyrd.
He thought the south was threatened most
From Normandy until he heard
Of Northern landings by a host
Of Vikings from Norway intent
On securing their King's own claim
To Harold's crown and to prevent
The Danes from doing just the same
Or waiting for the winds to bring
The Norman William to this land.
And Harold Hardrada, the King
Of Norway, had with him a band
Of rebel Northumbrians led
By Tostig. The exiled Earl, and
The brother of their King, had shed
With shame his pride and joined the hand
That held the landwaster, and spread

Beneath this flag was formed the grand
Array of Norway's might with men
From Isles of Orkney, Man, Shetland,
And Flemings, Scots and Irish. Ten
Thousand sea-wolves disgorged upon
The sands in Ricall's Crescent bay
And marched on York, their garrison
Of old, where Nordic Kings held sway
For centuries, and where the skill
In Skaldic verse once saved Egil,
The warrior peasant poet whose idyll
On Erick Blood-Axe's' life did fill
That king of York with such delight
He freed the man he swore to kill.
But now, two miles from York, the fight
For England's throne began. The shrill
Echoes of Mercian horns, the skirls
Of Northumbrian pipes gave cheer
To warriors of the Northern Earls
As they attacked with sword and spear
The sea wolves near the Fulford gate.
Edwin and Morca tried in vain
To stem the Viking flood. The fate
Of England lay amidst their slain.
Had they held back till Harold came
With reinforcements to their aid,
Their armies would have damped the flame
Of Viking dreams and would have made
The Normans reel from off the shore
At Pevensey, But now the two
Defeated brothers fought no more
And were not there when Harold slew
The sea wolves' King at Stamford Bridge
Or when the Normans killed their King

And sister's husband on the ridge
At Senlac. Yet firstly I must bring
You back to Yorkshire for the tale
Of Harold's victory. When he heard
The news of Fulford and the scale
Of Hardrada's invasion, word
Was sent to Each Hundred to call
The freemen out, the Fyrd, and gird
On arms for war and join the small
Devoted guard of House-Carl troops
As they progressed up Roman ways
Now overgrown and green. Some groups,
Who left the south, in just four days
Of gruelling toil, with Harold at
Their Head, covered some forty four
Odd miles per day. The House-Carls sat
On shaggy hog-maned mounts used more
For transport, seldom in a fight.
The Fyrd had ponies too, but most
Of Harold's men through day and night
Foot-slogged to reach the York out-post
Of Norwegians on Derwent side.
At Stamford Bridge the Viking host
Had let their normal caution slide
To rest and roast the ox and toast
Their battle feats with pride.
The southern armies swift advance
Surprised their king who thought they would
Be waiting for the threat from France
While he took hostages that should
Ensure his hold on York, impose,
Again, Tostig as rightful Lord
Of Northumbria and dispose
Of all his southern foes with sword

And fire from this old Viking base.
He was the greatest king of all
The Viking world and, of his race,
The bravest general and most tall.
He learnt his craft in Kiev's court
Of Yaroslav theWise, then down
The deep Dnieper sailed, and fought
In endless wars under the crown
Of Byzantium in with elite
Varangians. He crushed the foes
Of Emperors without defeat
In ten hard years. Despite the throes
Of war he quietly gathered gold
And silver, silks and jewels, the spoils
Of war to take back home and sold
To purchase power; For money oils
Ambitions wheels and easies man's
Desire to serve. On his return
In ten four five he shelved his plans
For England's throne. His first concern
Was for a slice of Norway, bought
For gold from Magnus who was killed
By accident quite soon, which brought
Hardrada, to the throne once filled
By king and saint Olaf, the stout,
His half brother whom he saw slain
At Stiklestad. With Magnus out
The way, the Danes elected Svein
As king and this meant certain war.
For Magnus (Hardrada's nephew)
Had won a war with Svein to bar
The Dane from rights that were his due
As nephew of Canute. For two
Decades this warfare raged until

A peace was made and both withdrew
To their own lands. With time to fill,
Hardrada had two years to plan
Invasion forces to campaign
Against England. But now this man,
This giant, this proud and ruthless King
Was taken by surprise, The guard
Upon the bridge fought hard to fling
The Saxon axemen off: but yard
By yard advanced as Vikings died
Until but one was left. This brave
Berserk, like Horatius, defied
The Saxon swords with skills to save
The bridge and give his King a chance
To muster all his men, and slew
The House Carls by the score. A lance
At last despatched this giant when through
The floor planks thrust, then Saxons swarmed
Across the bridge and gained the bank
And stormed the hollow square that formed
A hurried wall of shields of rank
On rank of desperate men. All day
The battle raged, and, as the sun
Declined so did the wall give way,
As ranks grew thin, and one by one,
Their leaders fell. First Tostig and
His rebel band, then Eyestein Orre,
Who'd guarded boats on Riccalls' sand,
Who led his men from off the shore
And ran to help his king; too late
He came and died in vain. The aim
Of Saxon bowmen sealed the fate
Of Viking dreams. The massive frame
Of Norway's King above the wall

Of shields could not be missed - he stood
With cleaving axe at seven feet tall,
And round him all his brother-hood
Of Royal Guards stood firm, The sun
Had nearly seen its day and still
The bloody battle raged and none
Could say who'd won the day until
A bowman's steady arm and eye
Dispatched an arrow into the throat
Of Norway's King. His axe held high
In one defiant stroke he smote
A House Carl dead, then, dying fell
Just like a crashing mighty oak.
His guard now knew he'd gone to dwell
In great Valhalla's Hall and broke
Into resounding cheers and knew
That they would join him there whom all,
In time, were killed. The Flemings flew
The field and few were left to call
The waverers back. In bright moon light
The scene became a sea-ward flight.
When Harold Godwin saw the sight
Of slaughter and the desperate plight
Of those remaining in the fight
He called a truce. And so the might
Of Norway and her polyglot
Allies were crushed for ever more.
He gave a solemn promise not
To land again on England's shore
And sailed away. And with them went
The younger sons of noble blood
Who had remained on shore and spent
Their waiting days with making good
The Viking boats. And one small Prince,

Hardrada's son, became the King,
Olaff the peaceful; others since
The Stamford Bridge defeat, the stripling
Viking war lords of Western Isles.
Three hundred boats had come to weigh
Their anchors at Riccall. And miles
Of bitter Northern seas now lay
Ahead for men who sailed away
In just two dozen boats with grey
War-weary wounded lain in hay
Or straw. Most of the boats would stay
In Riccalls bay, as deadmen cannot row
Or lift the sails, This hard fought war
Which Harold Godwin won, this blow
To Norway's pride, had left his corps
Of House Earl troops and Fyrd in need
Of rest and, with so many dead,
To find and train, with utmost speed,
Replacements good enough to head
Off threats from France. Down Ermine street
He sped with victory news. And then
He heard what he had feared. The fleet
From Norman ports had landed ten
Thousand men south of Haestingas
A province known of old to their
Forebears who came to harass
The coast in Alfred's time. One pair
Of Danish Vikings, Hastings and
The great Rollo, caused sore distress
And Hasting's brand remains on land
He seized. He built a strong fortress
At Milton. Descendants of those
Intrepid Norsemen chiefs now came
As Normans, back to fight so close

To Hastings Town whose very name
Was taken from the Danish Prince.
And branches of this Hastings tree
Have spread through England's history since
Those early days. In chivalry
In foreign wars, In court affairs
Baronial fights, intrigue, worship
And marriages to noble heirs,
In statesmanship and ownership
Of land, they played a powerful role
That brought them close to Scotland's stone
Of Scone and, through Catherine Pole,
Pretenders to the English throne.
Up here in Leicestershire they held
A great estate of which this park
Was part and many oaks were felled
To pay for Royal guests. And dark
The deed that fell on Hastings head
When Richard Crouchback came to reign.
But let us now pick up the thread
Of William's bid to claim and gain
The English throne and Harold's crown.
Now Harold made his rendezvous
Some sixty miles from London town
At Caldbeck Hill, and here he flew
The Wessex golden dragon flag
Which Edmund held with great renown
At Ashington. And on this crag
His famous 'fighting man' looked down
Upon the gathering weary troops.
In answer to their Kings command
Or to the Beacon fires, they came in groups
From distant shires to make their stand
Along with those from Stamford Bridge

On overgrown old Roman ways,
Or ancient tracks or Celtic ridge
Way paths, throughout October days
And nights they tramped or rode until
They saw the dragon flag and then
The 'fighting man' on Caldbeck Hill
And joined the King's own Wessex men.
King Harold knew he could not wait
For all his men to come, and those
Now there were tired and in no state
To launch a great attack. He chose
To find a ridge to hold his line
And give him time to rest his men,
Await reserves, and, at his sign,
To make a massive move. And when
He stood on Senlac Ridge he found
The place to make his stand and told
His army not to give up ground
Or break their ranks, but boldly hold
The line and steadfastly obey
Their King's command. So on Senlac
His army stood the thirteenth day
Of October to wait attack
From Hastings town. The ridge would guard
The route to London and would make
It hard for climbing men to ward
Off missiles from above, and break
A cavalry charge by Norman Knights.
His weary men lay down to rest;
And Norman spies would see the lights
And camp fire glow upon the crest
Of Senlac Ridge and, in disguise,
Have seen the preparations made
For war, the salient ridge, the size

Of Harold's force, fatigue displayed
And weapons held, and would apprise
The Duke of their intelligence.
He acted fast to gain surprise
Before the Saxon King's defence
Became too strong and made the prize
To hard to win, and by the dawn
Was on the march. Before the hour
Of ten his vast army was drawn
In battle lines against the flower
Of Saxon power. His centre troops
Were trusted Normans, while the right
Was held by Franco-Flemish groups
Of mercenaries and the might
Of Maine and Poitou and the knights
Of Brittany combined to hold
The left side flank beneath the heights
Of Senlac Ridge. The Bretons, bold
And Celtic to the core, were first
To charge the Saxon fold and feel
The angry missiles as they burst
Upon their ranks and made them reel
And stagger back. And then, despite
Their Kings command and battle plan,
Forsake their posts and ran to fight
The reeling foe. But nearly all
Were killed by arrows, axe or spear.
The Norman archers rained a fall
Of arrows on the Saxon army's rear
As infantry tried hard to dent
The forward House-Carl line, but still
The phalanx held; then William sent
In cavalry to charge the hill;
But, deep and boggy ground, and then

The slope and missiles slung, would tax
The strength of horse and man and when
The few got through, a Saxon axe
Would soon dispatch the lonely knight
To shouts of "out!" and "holy cross!".
All day the battle raged and right
Until one arrow caused the loss
Of Harold's life, the desperate fight
For England's crown was not resolved.
But that one arrow's deathly flight
Became the mortal blow that solved
The disputes end. When Harold fell
The Norman Duke sent word to all
His staff of Harold's death, to tell
Their troops the news and made a call
In them to make a final drive
To break the Saxon phalanx wall,
And take the Senlac Ridge and strive
To make the Saxons yield or fall
To Norman steel. When word was spread
He, standing in his stirrups tall
Upon his mare, lay bare his head
So all his men could see his face
And know he was not dead. For when
His horse had struck a boggy place
Unseating him, some worried men
Had whispered he was killed. His mace
He held up high then turned and led
His knights at a cantering pace
Towards the Senlac Ridge now red
With blood and strewn with dead in mounds.
The Horse-Carls fought until they died,
But levies fled to safer grounds
And groves and threw their swords and pride

Aside and rushed around like sheep
In droves without a shepherds care
To keep them safe from wolves. The sleep
Of death had claimed their king and there
Were few true leaders left to bring
The stragglers back. His brothers, Gyrth
And Leofwine lay with their king
Upon the bloody Senlac earth,
So William won by war the English throne
He once had claimed by his birth right
And Harold's death may now atone
His breaking a most solemn plight;
While England faced a sullen age,
An age of change and civil strife
Where power and order were the rage
For men who served a Noble's life:
A new and splendid time for those
Who ruled. An age for building stone
On stone, as great cathedrals rose,
And monasteries, to set the tone
Of Christian militancy; and grim,
Yet majestic, castles grew
To tame the countryside and trim
The weeds of discontent. A new
And feudal order stamped its feet
Upon the land while lords with strange
Un-English names and fine conceit
Began to make the Saxons change
Unruly ways, and treat their rights
With scant respect and cheat their lands
Away. The Norman court and knights
And sheriffs men and priests and bands
Of soldiers guarding towns all spoke
In Norman-French a tongue unknown

To Anglo-Saxon common folk
Who stubbornly refused to own
It as their own. Their language sprang
From old Germanic springs cognate
With ancient Norse with quite a tang
From Celtic streams with blends that date
From Roman founts and fresh the flow
From Norway's snow and water falls
And deep fiords that joined the slow
Related streams that crawls
From Danish plains. It has been said
That Anglo Saxons could converse
With ease on missions when they spread
The Christian word to wild perverse
Inhabitants of Viking lands
Beyond the sea. The language had
Evolved as all the racial strands
Entwined and still evolved to add
In words assimilated from
The Norman French and recognised
As middle English and become,
In time, English. When Christianised
The English Danes took on the tongue
The Anglo Saxons talked in speech, in song, with prayers;
In Latin too; the Normans did not prolong
Their speech for more than ninety years.
But words from every race remained
To grace the words of Chaucer, Gower
And Malory and England gained
A language which reflected power
And art, and history, church and state
And farm and hunting, travel, war
And peace and nature, love and hate
And music, stars and stage and honour

And death and all the fertile seeds
A Shakespeare needs to flower. I've told
A tale in great detail of deeds
Of ancient times because the mould
Of England's character was cast
To last for ever more in that
Old clay. The melting pot of past
Invasions has mixed inside the vat
Of life, a blood that flows with strains
Of Celtic moods and Roman sense,
Germanic strife, the restless Danes
The Norman French's eloquence
To give a British race its strange
Distinctive character, its grace,
That has not suffered serious change
Since Chaucer's death took place.

A MODERN SAGA

Norway 1940, while with 5th Battalion the Leicestershire Regiment

The tale I tell is true, a sort
Of saga, sad in parts, that tells
Of what befell my men who fought
A war around the Neverjells.
And how they lost and lived and sought
Refuge; of shame, and shock and shells.
From Nevra's glassy ski resort
The German songs were gay and loud
And echoed round the mountain fells.
They had good reason to be proud
And sing and drink that night. They knew
Their martial skills had won the day
From Oslo through to Ringebu,
And Quisling soon would have his way;
And Norway slowly bled and cried
For aid, quite unprepared to keep
Their country free and stem the tide
Of Nazi greed. No time to sleep
Bewildered, beaten, tired, the brave
Norwegian soldiers fought with pride
Compelled to fall back fighting wave
On wave of hardened troops. They tried
To emulate the Finns whose lean
And tiny army ran circles round
The massive Russian war machine
By brilliant use of men and ground,
But Finland had no quisling germ
To spread a plague of doubt and fear

And had prepared and had stood firm
Against all odds for all that year.
Yet Norway's king with scorn defied
Attempts upon his life and throne
And roughed it by his army's side
And never left the battle zone.
The German staff by one bold stroke
Had gained advantage of surprise;
It was too late when Britain woke
To counteract this enterprise.
Their Cabinet of war went mad,
Remembered Munich, Prague, Warsaw,
And wondered if they had to add
In Oslo's name for Lord Haw Haw
To sneer across the air as yet
Another sign of impotence.
In their resolve to act they let
Their hearts decide what common sense
Denied, to send an army force
Across the sea to help Norway.
The Generals had to act, of course;
But sought in vain for some delay
To plan, equip and properly train
A ski-brigade for mountain snow,
Essential for a sound campaign;
And we were sent in haste to show
The flag and boarded *Devonshire*
In pensive yet in happy mood.
And all the stores we would require
Were stacked with care, the ammo, food
And spares well packed in holds below;
And then, when all was quiet and calm,
The order came for us to go
On shore again With much alarm

And rumours rife, we moved to great
Orion at berth beneath the spans
Of Bridge of Forth, and almost straight
Away were disembarked as plans
Where changed again, our unit split
To fit inside much smaller craft
Like sardines in a tin. Out stores and kit
Went to and fro and fore and aft
And spread about on every boat.
It seemed Lord Haw Haw, at his best,
Had got our masters by the throat,
And stirred up quite a hornet's nest
When heard, sarcastically, to gloat
Of German bombers coming soon
To sink the ships and troops afloat
The Forth. Because there was a moon
That cloudless April night this meant
The Bridge and huge *Orion* would be
At risk and she was swiftly sent
Away while we prepared for sea
On board the *Curacoa*. This tale
Of chaos, of confusion worse
Confounded, this perplexed wholesale
Ineptitude brought down a curse
On this campaign which damned it right
From start to end. We bore the brunt;
But not the blame and had to fight
Incompetence on Whitehall's front
Before we even left these shores.
We disembarked at Andlesness
And tried to find essential stores
Mislaid, miscarried, in the mess
At Rosyth; but far too much had gone
Astray. In fact we were no more

The well equipped Battalion
That trained so hard on Raby Moor.
An then we heard bad news to crown
Our cursed luck - that all transport
And artillery had gone down
When *Cedar Bank* was sunk just short
Of Norway's coast. We had been sent
To fight, and fight we would. We came
With willing hearts and good intent;
But, to our everlasting shame,
So ill-equipped for snow warfare,
So ignorant of how to cope
With endless trees, quite unaware
Of mountain ways; we had no hope
Of air-support or tanks or guns;
Our mortar bombs were lost at sea,
So all we had against the Huns
Were brens and rifles. Within three
Frustrated days we faced the test
Of fire as we relieved the brave
Dragoons withdrawing for a rest.
In waist-deep snow we stood and gave
No ground and kept a steady fire
On Alpine troops but yards ahead.
Our line was like a funeral pyre
Ablaze from bombs the Stuka's shed
In screaming dives of death, and lead
From spitting Messerschmitts unfrocked
The trees and turned the snow to red.
The road to Arneberg was blocked
With fallen timber which became
A mass of flame that spread from tree
To tree and made an easy aim
For German field artillery

And planes and deadly mortar fire.
For seven hours a battle raged
An then, on orders to retire
To higher ground, we slowly staged
A planned withdrawal The only way
To climb the hill was by the road;
The woods were thick and snow there lay
Too deep and soft. This episode
Of our withdrawal will stay with me
As long as life shall last. The four
Inch mortars were, I'm sure, the key
To German victory, worth more
To infantry for close support
Than planes or guns. We felt like stack
Yard rats enclosed in mesh and caught
Without the means of fighting back.
They got our range and as we climbed
They raised their sights. We heard
The mortars fire their bombs and timed
Our dives to ground before they whirr'd
From out the sky and burst in shreds
Of shrapnel where we lay. We played
This game with death and kept our heads
Until we reached the crest and made
Defences on the hill. But, sad
To say, in that long haul two men
Were killed and several more had
Bad wounds and could not walk, and when
We backed an ambulance down hill
To gather them, the barrage stilled
For long enough for us to fill
It and return. The cold air chilled
Us to the bone, but lighting wood
For food and warmth would have been

Unwise because the Germans could
Not fail to aim at smoke then seen
And bomb the buildings where a few
Norwegians lived; they had refused
To leave their wooden homes. We drew
Our rations, sparse and cold, and used
Our rum to warm our weary bones.
Then orders came to move once more
Towards Asmark. We heard the groans
Of tanks not far away, the roar
Of engines stuck in snow, and then
When on the march, the sudden zooms
Of fighter planes and saw the frozen
Surface of the road pop up plumes
Of ice as bullets beat their lead
Tattoos along our path. When they
Uncurled from dives, just over-head
And low, we fired our brens away
And aimed our rifles at the planes;
And how we cheered when one was hit
And spurted smoke and flames! The strains
Of war began to show a bit,
And men were tired through lack of sleep
And food and constant moves, and yet
Morale was high. Not all could keep
Up with the pace and I was met
By Colonel Guy and he told me
To hurry back and whip in all
The waverers for "they must be,"
He said, "though some may have to crawl,
Across the Lillehamer bridge
By six o'clock for then it would
Be blown; and make for Faberg ridge,
Our new defensive line" (the good

And brave C.O. I never saw
In that campaign again. He fought
Against all odds a futile war,
Was over run, cut off and caught).
I gathered up my weary flock
And made them move, but still too slow
To beat the time. At six o'clock
We heard a thunderous boom echo
Around the hills and knew our chance
Had gone. And as we went down toward
The town we passed an ambulance
And several lorries burning hard.
I hid my men inside a wood
And with my batman-runner made
A reconnaissance. One house stood
Out from the rest for this displayed
A large red-cross upon its roof.
We walked towards this house and saw
A sight which gave us all the proof
Required to know a German corps
Was in the town. A long convoy
Of open trucks in which sat men
Upright and stiff and grim like toy
Tin soldiers on review. We then
Entered the hospital and sought
For news of British troops. A tall
And beaming orderly then brought
Us milk and said he knew that all
The town was German now and we
Should stay, and wait for his return
To bring us help and keep us free
From harm. But soon, with grave concern
A pretty nurse came up to me
And warned us that the man had run

To fetch the Huns. He was a key
Nazi, the Quisling number one
Of Lillehamer. I thanked this good
And loyal nurse with all my heart
And asked if she could find us food
To take away with us. A trolley cart
With bread and cheese was then brought out
And these were loaded in our packs.
Her final act was then to scout
Outside and mark my map with tracks
To take to reach the path that led
To Maihaugen, a mountain ski
Resort. I found the men and fed
Them best I could, and saw that we
Had now been joined by other men
And was relieved to see that three
Of these were officers and ten
Were other ranks. We made some tea
In our mess-tins and then, in files,
Set off to find the mountain trail.
We'd walked that day some twenty miles
And found the mountain tough to scale
With all our heavy packs and guns
And lack of sleep and soaking feet;
And snow up to our thighs made one's
Advance up hill a slogging feat
Of pure resolve. As we got near
The top a bonny maid with flaxen hair,
A Nordic Siren mountaineer,
Sat waiting in a rocky lair,
And handed Tony Cripps a note
In English. "Follow this girl and she
Will lead you safely here". "Who wrote
This note?" the Captain asked, but he

Got no reply. In German, then
In French, he tried in vain. He went
Ahead with her and said that when
He blew his whistle loud, and sent
Her back with map and gloves we'd know
It was no trap. We waited till
The signal came and down the snow
The maiden slid, and what a thrill
It was to reach the sun-clad crown.
Norwegians, all in ski-ing gear,
Forgot there was a war and down
The slopes they weaved in sheer
Exuberance, which we thought,
And said, was odd, and hardly fair
On fighting men. "But most were caught
On holiday, and did not dare
To travel home, "an old man said,
(It was his note we got) "yet some,"
He cried "have not been taught to tread
The path of honour and become
Devoid of duty." He then gave
Us food and went to find a truck
To take us further north and save
Us walking in the snow. With luck,
He thought, we could catch up with our
Own troops. He soon returned with two
Old army trucks of doubtful power.
We thanked our host who was a true
Norwegian patriot, and left
And drove across a wide plateau;
The sky was clear, the land bereft
Of trees and all we saw was snow
And mountain peaks and peace did reign.
We knew, somehow, our luck was bound

To change and suddenly a plane,
Whose sound we had not heard came round
A peak so low I saw the face
Inside the cockpit overhead
Look down as if he wished to trace
If we were friend or foe, then sped
Away about a mile then made
A slow deliberate turn. We thumped
The drivers cab with fists and bade
Him stop as off the truck we jumped.
As sailors swim from sinking ships
So we, in panic, tried to stride
Away with snow up to our hips
To flop in waves of drifts and hide,
We hoped, from harm. And when he came
The bullets struck a truck inside
And broke the wooden roof-span frame.
We told the men to spread out wide
And well away from what now stood
As sitting ducks. The plane returned
And set alight the canvas hood
Of both the trucks. And as they burned
He flew away. We ran to rip
The blazing canvas down and throw
Up snow to smother flames and strip
Away the wooden seats aglow
Where we had sat. The keys were turned,
The engines churned and off we went
Again. And three more times we learned
To dance with death and circumvent
The straffing plane. But in the last
Attack a petrol tank was hit
And with a blast lit up and cast
Us into gloom. We had to fit

The men in one remaining truck,
And left out packs behind to gain
The standing space required, and, stuck
Together tight, we took the strain
And crabwise crawled to reach a high
Hotel they named Nevra by four
o'clock. Again, we wondered why
So many people skied and bore
So little empathy with their
Compatriots at war. They gave
Us Smorgasbord and beer
And rooms in which to wash and shave
And promised us a mighty meal
That night and feather beds to sleep
Upon. They would, for us, repeal
The law Norwegians had to keep
"No liquor during war," unseal
The wine cellar and drink our health.
I doubt our men had ever seen
Such luxury before, such wealth,
Such kindness showered on them or been
Inside so wonderful a place.
But soon our dreams of rest received
A sudden jolt. We had to face
Unpleasant facts. We had deceived
Ourselves and really could not blame
The crisis that arose upon
Our hosts. A Swedish Colonel came
Upstairs to us where we had gone
To wash. His face was pale and grave.
He clicked his heels and bowed, and said,
As Officers we must behave
And act with honour and not shed
Civilian blood! If we stayed

In Nevra, Germans would release
Their bombs upon the place, and prayed
That we would leave forthwith and cease
Our selfish ways! It was quite true
That Nevra was a holiday
Resort with children there. We knew
We had to go without delay.
Upon the ski-ing coat he wore,
The Colonel had a fine display
Of campaign ribbons which he swore
He'd earned in France in World War One.
In Canada when just a lad
He'd joined the ranks and fought the Hun
Upon the Somme. He said he had
Just sewn the ribbons on to prove
He was for us. He said we ought
To walk about six miles and move
Into some mountain huts he thought
Beyond the reach of German ski
Patrols. He would provide a guide
To take us there and come to see
What else we might require. We tied
Supplies on sledges, our target
Was Hundersetter; but had we
Perceived what lay ahead, the sweat
And stress and toil and misery,
Perhaps we would have planned a less
Exhausting route to take. The snow
Was like quick-sand and our progress
A slow wallowing plod of woe.
When looking back I can recall
Five years of war, all overseas,
This was the very worst of all
The marches that I made. Burmese

Campaigns were cruel and tough;
Somaliland was hot and dry;
And Abyssinia quite rough enough;
But none of these campaigns did try
My strength and will as did this bit
Of Norway's snow, when just to lift
One's legs became a trial. Though fit
And young I must admit each drift
I sank into thigh-deep I thought
I could curl down right there, and sleep,
Or die, I did not care I fought
This apathy somehow to keep
Alive and beat this arctic waste.
And when we reached the huts at last
We were so tired we could not taste
The salted fish or rich repast
The Nevra chef had packed in haste.
We ticked off names as men went past
The gate all wet up to the waist,
Exhausted, cold but not downcast,
And allocated each a hut
To share, and gave them tea and made
Them change their socks. All but
A few reported in and aid
Was sought from guides who found them all
And brought them in before frost-bite
Had taken toll. The whole roll-call
Complete, we went inside to light
The stove, removed our boots, and lay
Upon the floor and soundly slept.
It snowed without a break next day
And we were pleased the wind had swept
Our tracks away. We asked our guide
To find us skis and this he did.

We dare not go, by day, outside
As planes were overhead; but hid
Inside the huts. But when the moon
Was bright at night we learnt in style
To ski the slopes and very soon
Became quite good. We went a mile
Uphill one night in line to test
The skins we might require to climb
The mountain sides. We had the best
Instruction possible in time
Of war from four Norwegian men;
And Colonel Jansen helped a lot
And gave us good advice. And when
He told us Germans had just shot
Civilians who had helped to hide
An Englishman, and some had dined
At his Hotel, we knew the tide
Had turned. That starry night we lined
Up all the men and skied about
Ten miles of icy wind and snow.
It was our fist big trip without
A guide. We were too large and slow
But got to Skollasetter where,
We had been told, was food. When we
Got there we found the cupboards bare
And not a thing to eat. The tea
We brought with us we brewed, and lay
Inside the huts awhile to rest
And wax our skis and plan the way
To go, north, east or west. The quest
For food was critical. Our map
Revealed the next homestead would take
A night to reach without mishap.
And was there food? For safety's sake

We thought it wisest to retrace
Our tracks, hungry, depressed and tired.
And when we rolled up at our base
We found the huts had been acquired
By Forresters of our Brigade
Two Officers and a platoon
Of men. We called our last parade
Next day at dawn and said, by noon,
They must divide themselves in small
 Self-chosen groups of four or five.
We would then share amongst them all
Sufficient food to say alive
For several days; each group would take
A compass, rucksack, map and cash.
At night we'd tell each group to make
A break on every hour and dash
For cover of tile trees. A guide
Had gone to Nevra for supplies
And these we would with care divide
Among the groups. We said disguise
Of any sort was far from wise
Because they could be shot as spies
If caught and also did advise
It best to keep off roads or near
The towns, and if they could not reach
Our troops up north they must steer
A course due east to Sweden. Each
Man, we said, had done his best
And no-one need feel ashamed;
They had all passed the toughest test
Of fire and stress and now had tamed
The terrors of the snow by skill
On skis and this should ease their way
All through the night the drill

We'd planned and practised all the day
Achieved its aim without a hitch.
The Officers were last to go in two
Odd groups. They had debated which
Was best, to lead a group, undo,
In other words, the choice to choose
One's friends; or, as this choice applied
To all, they thought they would not lose
Respect if they were satisfied
To stay a group of friends. They too
Had done their duty to their men
And seen them safely off with true
Concern and basic needs. As when
Upon a sinking ship the cry
"Abandon Ship" is called the last
To leave are Officers who try
To see that all their men have cast
Themselves to sea, that rafts are free
And boats are lowered. We then said
Farewell to guides, Jansen and three
Norwegian girls who brought us bread
And milk and cheese each night at risk
Of being caught and shot. The snow
Was falling fast; our pace was brisk
As we departed keen to show
We were not beaten yet. And so
A trek of fourteen days began
Towards the north. Some days we'd go
Without a meal or share a can
Of bully beef or split a small
Anchovy tin in five. Some nights
We'd break our rule and make a call
On valley farms if we saw lights
And ask for food. But on the whole

We found our food where setters sat
On hills - the summer farms. We stole
From these the hams and cheese and fat
In pans we rubbed on boots to seal
Them water tight. We stole to live
And lived to eat. For every meal
We had to fight and win or give
In. Our desperate craving released
A latent force to drive us through
The barrier of pain; increased
Our will to thrive and helped renew
Our confidence. We crossed a white
Plateau one day into the wind
And sun. The glare reflected bright
From snow and I was left behind
Next day with snow-blindness and had
To lie for several days supine
In darkness, pain, and very sad
And sorry for myself. A fine
Fenrik, Eric Von Krogh, was there
With some Norwegian troops and they
Were very kind to me. I swear
He saved my sight. One stormy day
He skied to Ringebu to find
A chemist shop and found the town
In German hands. He hid behind
A barn until the sun went down
Then, like a thief, he slunk and crept
Around the streets until he found
A pharmacy. The chemist slept
Above his shop; but he was bound
To open up if someone pressed
The night-bell for emergent needs.
Von Krogh then told his tale and stressed

How much these dark and desperate deeds
Must never be revealed. The brave
Fenrick returned in blinding snow
With cocaine drops the chemist gave
To him to cure my eyes. I know
He travelled thirteen miles that night
On skis and risked his life for me,
And thanks to him my normal sight
Was soon restored and I could see
To thank him eye to eye. Nothing
Could dim the gratitude I felt
For him. My winter turned to spring
And all my gloom began to melt
And faith and hope returned. This group
Of men were part of number two
Oppland, a cavalry-ski troop
Of eighty men who had been through
The fighting in the south and, cut
Off from their squadron, now prepared
To move up north. And in my hut
Their Doctor dwelt. He nursed and cared
For me and sent Von Krogh to get
The drops. His name was Humerfelt
A name I never will forget.
He travelled around the hills and dealt
With wounds and mental scars and trained
His orderlies in first-aid work.
Within a week the fates ordained
To change my luck and perk
Me up no end. I heard a shout
Outside and saw my friends were there.
We had agreed that if one fell out
The others must go on and spare
No thought and waste no time on one

Who could not keep up with the rest.
Apparently the group had done
Their best to reach our troops north west
Of Dombas when they heard that all
The British force had been got out
Of Norway safe. With this withdrawal
They turned about and had no doubt
That Sweden to the East should be
The next priority. And Guy,
The Colonel, had been caught and three
Of our best friends were killed and nigh
On half the Regiment had not made
The voyage home. We went our way
To Sweden very much afraid
We may be captured yet. By day
We slept, at night we skied and had
Our moments of despair, of fun, and near
Escapes and rows, and when the mad
Desire for food was great, the fear
Of being caught became far less
Than fears of running out of food,
And there were times, I must confess,
I fell into a sombre mood
Of deepest gloom. Near Hanestead
We found Reg Coleman and a guide
Who helped to plan our route ahead.
There was no longer need to hide
By day, the country was so bleak
And bare which made our food more
Hard to find. It took a week
To trek the hundred miles before
We reached the Swedish line to be
Interned for several months then sent
To Finland and across the sea

To England and our Regiment,
And fight again our enemy.

Note

1.	Colonel Guy German, commanded I/5 Battalion Leicestershire Regiment T.A. He was awarded a D.S.O. for his bravery and leadership in Norway. He spent most of the rest of the War in German P.O.W. camps mainly the notorious Colditz Castle, where he was senior British Officer. His brother John was my Company Commander and was killed in Normandy. Their father, Colonel John German, had previously commanded the same Battalion.

2.	Major M. A. L. Cripps D.S.O. served later in other campaigns with the Regiment. Now a Q.C. and has been Recorder of Nottinghamshire. He married Colonel Scott's sister.

3.	Major R. G. Coleman was awarded the Norwegian M.C. with sword, for his bravery in Norway.

4.	Dr Sigurd Humerfclt was medical officer to Squadron Regiment Oppland No.2 under Col. J. M. Aamodt. He worked after the war as a Doctor in various towns in Norway. He went back to the Army in 1945 to look after 18,000 Russian prisoners at Trondheim. When last heard of (1968) he was Professor of Dept. A of the Medical Department of the University of Bergen.

5.	Erik Von Krogh. He was a Fenrick (a 2nd Lieutenant) with the same Regiment as the Doctor above. After the War he became a Commercial Artist. His last known address (1968) was Nedre Skoguei 4, Oslo 2.

6.	A few guides and helpers I have names of are:- Rolf Falkenberg- Smith. He used to work in Bennetts Travel Bureau, Oslo. Dan Halfamstrom, Den Norskercredit Bank, Oslo. Einar Houdhaugen 2632 Venebygd

7.   The two Officers killed were Captain Jim Ford-Smith, Adjutant, and Captain "Heckie" Ramsden, M.C. They are buried at Lillehamer with about 35 other graves of British Soldiers, eight of our Battalion.

8.   The other officers of our group were:-

        i) Douglas Asbury, later Colonel. He was very brave in Norway particularly in operating a Bren gun on a tripod mounted on a truck, against the planes quite regardless of his own safety.

        ii) Raymond Savage. Captain Savage and I were the youngest 2nd Lieutenants. 1 think we were both about 20 years old at the time He later spent 4 years in a Jap P.O.W. Camp. He married my cousin.

        iii) Captain Ernest Scott. Later Colonel Scott O.B.E. who married my cousin Rosamund Moore whose father and brother both got M.C.s in my Regiment Captain Roger Barratt, Adjutant after Ford-Smith was killed.

9.   All the groups got to Sweden. We were the first to cross the border. All of us were interned at Falun which was like any POW camp, with barbed wire and sentry posts at corners. Inside the camp we ran the show ourselves, kept discipline and ran work parties, growing our own vegetables etc. One camp Commandant was Col. Tennant of the Green Howards, I think.

10.   Nevra Hotel. A few years ago I went back to Norway, having booked into the Nevra Hotel with my wife and family. The Swedish Colonel's actual words were "If you do not leave, the place will be a , shell of fire and broken children". On our arrival at the Hotel, having driven up from Oslo, we found to my horror that the place was a "shell of fire" and had just suffered the worst Hotel fire in Norway's history (so I was told). We had to go elsewhere. I hear it has been rebuilt.

11.   Hundersetter is now part of the Pellestova ski resort run by Mr

Pelle Skalinstad who helped us in 1940.

THE BALLAD OF BROOKLET FARM
- 'a fantasy'

A sporting tale of local charm
Is found recorded by the Squire
At Isley Walton, Leicestershire,
Upon a barn at Brooklet Farm.
The slab of stone is carved with skill,
The message is a hunting lore
That tells of eighteen forty four
When hounds went home without a kill.
They met in Donington's old grounds
Where Celt and Roman, Saxon, Dane
And Normans in the past have slain
The boar and deer and fox with hounds,
And where the Domesday Oaks still grow
Around Lord Hastings's Gothic Hall
Which stands so proud, pristine and tall,
The hounds still hunt as long, ago.
That day, they drew the Quarry Wood
And found a fox and hounds spoke well
And ran it Fast to Nancy's dell;
The mist had gone and scent was good.
And hounds like running water streamed
Across the turf and, as a water fall
With speckled surf, across the wall
They poured and into Dalbys screamed.
As Hastings's Marquis past his seat
A happy man was he to be
The Master of such hounds and see
Such stamina and speed, and sweet
Their music to his ears. He Wound
His horn that hunting morn as well

As any huntsman born to swell
The splendid symphony of sound
The fox ran straight to Coppice Lodge
Where keeper kept his pheasant pens
And fighting cocks and bantam hens,
And here began to weave and dodge
The land upon these rearing grounds
Was foiled and all the hounds at fault;
The hunt had come to sudden halt
Till master came, caught hold his hounds
And lifted them to Starkey's hill
And cast them carefully with skill.
They feathered down the field until
Old Flora, near the Studbrook rill
Hit line and boldly threw her tongue
And others knew the bitch spoke true
And wheeled towards her scenting clue,
And soon the solid pack had swung
To share her find. The Marquis blew
The veline on his horn and blessed
Old Flora's magic nose and pressed
His spurs to heaving flanks and flew
Behind his pack to Brooklet Farm.
The fox, on reaching there, espied
A ladder leaning up the side
Of Brooklet Barn and chanced his arm,
And climbed inside the loft with guile;
And while he lay in soft old hay
He heard the hounds begin to bay
Below his hide. In lurcher style
They sought their prey, became unwise
And used their eyes to scan the ricks
And stacks of straw and heaps of sticks,

And sheds of drays and Tamworth sties,
And stores of sacks and tools and twine,
And generally behaved as bad
As any Tinker's cur, and sad
It was to see old Herod's line
Disgrace his blood. No well-bred hounds
Should sight a fox, but only wind
His scent, and these, regrettably, had sinned
And Master's fury knew no bounds.
This Master of Lord Hastings's hunt
Was proud of his great name and spent
The winters of his life content
To ride to hounds and rode in front
And feared no fall. He took pride
In tenants' farms and always cried
When any of their children died;
And for their old age would provide;
He never raised their rents at all.
He seldom saw his wife by day
And even less by night. They say
He was so kind of heart he'd call
To visit sleeping maids to warm
Their beds and stroke their heads and calm
Their ghostly fears, and softly charm
Away their tears, or rub with balm
Their wheezing chests. The only sins
In this good man of mighty girth
Were those that ran with noble birth
And Country Squires with double chins,
The sins of gluttony and greed.
These made them stout and prone to gout
And apt to blow their brains about,
Or die at table as they feed.

He dined on devilled kidneys done
In aspic, venison and veal,
And salmon from the Trent, and eel,
And suckling pig and ham and one
Big pie of pigeon, rook and hare;
And partridge, pheasant, all well hung;
And plover's eggs and rabbits young,
And grouse from Loudoun, beef so rare;
The tongues of larks and stilton ripe.
All this he'd eat and wash well down
With ale and wine, enough to drown
A dryft of swine, and then a pipe
Of shag or long havana take;
Perhaps a pinch of snuff, then cup
His brandy bowl in palms and up
The stairs by candle light to make
His altruistic rounds. At dawn
He rose each hunting morn and went
To chapel prayers and prayed for scent,
Then downed some ale and beef and brawn,
Then to his lawn to mount his mare
Just like he did that very day
Which ended in such disarray
And turned his noble head of hair
To grey. For when he saw the scene
Described he rated hounds full hard
And swore such words that, in the yard,
The labourers in their smocks were seen
To blush with shame. The dairy maid
Fell off her stool and with a wail
Upset her pail and went as pale
As milk she spilt. The pigman stayed
Inside his sty and shivered cold

With fear. The shepherd could not bear
To hear such awful swearing near
His sheep so knelt inside his fold,
Put down his crook, and covered up
His ears and bleated like a lamb.
His sheep went mad and ran and swam
Into the pond. His collie dog and pup
Became insane and, with a yell,
Disappeared inside the well.
The cowman tried his best to quell
The bolting bullocks, but he fell
Among his steers and there he lay
Until next day well trodden in
The dung. The Farmer's ruddy skin
Had turned from red to ashen grey,
He hung his head and tore his hair
And foamed about the mouth. His wife
In screaming panic fled for life
And locked the cellar door and there
She sat upon the stairs and sipped
Her rhubarb wine until she saw
All things in pairs, began to caw
A Jackdaw cry and slowly slipped
On to the floor. The ploughman knew
The squires boom and thought his hour
Had come. His team of shires and plough,
Like two year olds, in terror flew
A hedge and out of view. He gave
An awful scream and threw his hat
Upon the ground and jumped on that,
Then sat upon the soil to rave
And howl as he was apt to do
At night when harvest moon was new.

THE PROSTITUTE'S PROGRESS

With apologies to Hogarth's 'Rakes Progress'

Condemn me as a Courtesan,
Deplore my ancient trade,
Degrade me as a Citizen,
I am as I was made.
    With Dad in jail for many years
    My Mum went 'on the game,'
    I grew up wise in street affairs
    Bereft of love and shame.
I knew neglect, abuse and tears,
The ways of waifs and strays,
I knew the fears of rent arrears;
But never holidays.
    My granny paid towards my school
    A long bus ride away,
    With super Gym and Swimming pool
    And many games to play.
The other girls were sweet to see
Like roses gently born;
But few were ever kind to me
And scoffed at me with scorn.
    My petals went with child abuse
    And childhood innocence.
    My thorn remained and came in use
    When needed in defence.
I tried, in vain, to prick the vein
That pumped their precious pride;
I tried to pierce their pomp and drain
The hate away inside.
    I was expelled for petty crimes
    And sent to schools elsewhere;
    But I absconded several times
    And ended up 'in care.'

The home in which I served my time
Was no 'New-Leaf' retreat;
But more a school of lust and crime
For sweepings of the street.
>I learnt to steal from jewellery stores,
>And where to fence my take.
>I learnt to open locks and doors
>With special keys I'd make.
Sometimes it paid to be a pair
And I would take a mate.
We'd 'case each joint' with utmost care
And risks investigate.
>We watched the way the cameras stalked,
>And where they zoomed and why,
>And where the store detectives walked
>And where they gloomed to spy.
We knew the harm a shop alarm
Can cause to such as we;
But had the knowledge to disarm
This threat to liberty.
>We went, at intervals, inside
>The shop to pluck and palm,
>And I would be a blushing bride
>And smile with nubile charm.
I'd ask to see a jewellery tray
Of rings and filigrees,
My friend would faint and pass away,
Her skirt above her knees.
>The salesman sank upon the floor
>To help the stricken maid.
>I quietly locked the entrance door
>And said I'd phoned for aid.
He fingered free her buttoned dress
As she began to groan,
And as his hands began to press

Her groan became a moan.
　　　　He was too busy saving life
　　　　To bother watching me,
　　　　I did not ring, but used my knife
　　　　To cut security.
The salesman thought she may expire
And blew inside her throat,
I cut the throat of every wire
And then took off my coat.
　　　　I placed it on his nodding head
　　　　And covered up his eyes
　　　　We tied his hands with twisted thread
　　　　Ignoring all his cries.
And loaded up the gems and rings
From off the jewellery tray,
And lifted other precious things
To crown our palmy day.
　　　　I thought I never could be caught
　　　　Or come to any harm
　　　　I thought all policemen could be bought
　　　　Or fall for female charm.
But not all Bobbies on the beat
Are 'bent' or 'on the take';
Once caught red-handed in the street
I made my big mistake.
　　　　When apprehended at this crime
　　　　My usual ploys all failed,
　　　　No smiles, beguiles or bribes this time
　　　　Could stop me being jailed
It was a female Cop, you see,
Immune to bribes or tears
Who clamped the clicking cuffs on me
And 'put me down' for years.
　　　　Redemption there could not be found
　　　　To mend my wilful ways;

My prison was a breeding ground
    For perverts, pimps and gays.
Before I was so clearly caught
And carted off to 'Jug'
I'd always fought against the thought
Of taking any Drug.
    One knows one's judgement is impaired
    When driving after drink;
    This principle I fully shared
    Before I went to 'Clink.'
I could not rob if full of 'Speed'
Or do a job on 'Coke';
I never even felt the need
To sniff at things or smoke.
    In jail the Barons ruled the trade
    On such a fearsome scale
    That debts were paid and fortunes made
    By all the drugs on sale.
Abstainers did not last too long
As bullies forced the pace;
One had to buy 'just to belong'
Or get a 'razor face.'
    And now I'm free of noxious weeds
    And steal no more or cheat;
    Instead I satisfy the needs
    Of those whose hurts I treat.
For men with cold or frigid wives
I serve a desperate need,
And some, with sad and sex-starved lives,
Their appetite I feed.
    I am a sort of safety valve
    Releasing pent up steam
    From bursting heat, The soothing Salve
    For sensual wounds, The Cream.
To comfort lonely souls and sad

Inadequates, the weak
The warped, the shamed, the shy, the bad,
The lost, the lame, and meek
  I'm sure there would be less abuse
  And less domestic strife
  If Doctors could prescribe our use
  For frustration's ills in life.
Some see me as a bird of prey
That scours the urban street
To pick up rotten flesh the way
A vulture cleans the bones of meat.
  Some whores are 'tarty' in their dress
  And loud as they are lewd;
  Their scent is cheap, their hair a mess
  Their speech is crude and rude.
I earn my rent and daily bread
And save for rainy days
By being very good in bed,
And knowing clients ways.
  I never flash my sex about
  Or greet men in the street,
  I never wave down cars or shout,
  Or walk a special beat.
I have no cards in seedy stores
But use a mobile 'phone.
I never share with other whores
And live, in style, alone.
  I use my mobile 'phone to meet
  The men who come to me;
  My dress is classic and discreet
  As though they've come for tea.
But most who ring have been before
I know what games to play;
But some I've banned and come no more
No matter what they pay.

And who can judge what's wrong or right
>Inside this moral maze?
>And who can tell what's black and white
>When all one sees are greys?
And who is pure of sin in heart
With hands so clean of guilt,
That he can cast the stone to start
Destroying what God built?
>For He built me and all mankind,
>And gave us light and shade
>And gave each one a trade to find
>**I am as I was made.**

*This was written after hearing on the news that some **female** students were going*
'on the game!' to pay their fees. I thought it wrong that well educated ladies
should take the work from girls on council estates caught in the poverty trap with
no education or work.

Weemabah, N.S.W.

On the occasion of the Marriage of
Natasha Mack to Gareth Evans

<u>11th APRIL 1998</u>

*Natasha Jane Mack, cousin of Cynthia Moore who married my cousin
Peter. I became her friend after first meeting on Rutland Polo Ground
1993.It was five years later we discovered she was cousin to my cousin's
wife. Cynthia was the daughter of Dr Mason of Tumut N.S.W. cousin of
the Macks.*

So far away across the sea
The champagne and the caviar
Salute the bride of 'Weemabah'
Just joined in wedlock at Trangie.
Gareth, the groom, has caught a bride
The brightest star in heaven above
Who fell to earth to be his love
And tie perfection to his side.
The name of Gareth Evans hails
From mountain vales and salmon streams
Where Chapel Choirs and Rugby Teams
Wear leeks on David's day in Wales.
Natasha Jane will have to train
To live on leeks and learn the way
The Cymric cook and how to play
The harp and sing; yet still remain
An Aussie Mach and harmonise
Old Celtic lore with those of New
South Wales. I bid you fond adieu
Natasha Mack, as paradise
Becomes your prize. I pray, one day
You may return to sip champagne

On Rutland Polo fields again
And see your English friends at play.
And now, I plea for one request
As I close down this humble verse,
That we should still be friends and nurse
Our friendship so it stands the test
Of time and distant climes. Depend
On friends, for life is short and full
Of change and days are bright and dull
But constant is a loving friend.

Sept 1999